NATIONAL GEOGRAPHIC GUIDE TO

The World's Secret Places

Vibrantly colored wildflower
blooms decorate a field in
Alentejo, Portugal.

NATIONAL GEOGRAPHIC GUIDE TO

The World's Secret Places

ESCAPES TO UNSPOILED
AND UNDISCOVERED EARTHLY PARADISES

by David Yeadon

NATIONAL GEOGRAPHIC
WASHINGTON, D.C.

A serene vista creates ambience at a café in Saint-Cirq Lapopie, France.

Contents

ARCTIC

NORTH

AMERICA

Seeley-Swan Valley
Montana
USA

Hells Canyon
Idaho-Oregon border
USA

Sand Hills
Nebraska
USA

Green Mountains
Vermont
USA

Grand Manan
New Brunswick
CANADA

Vinalhaven
Maine
USA

Harris
Isle of Lewis
Scotland
UNITED KINGDOM

Dorset
England
UNITED KINGDOM

Lot & Cele Valleys
FRANCE

Galicia
SPAIN

Pyrenees-
Basque
FRANCE

Alentejo
PORTUGAL

São Miguel
Azores
PORTUGAL

Atlas
Mountains
MOROCCO

Gomera
Canary Islands
SPAIN

Îles des Saintes
Guadeloupe
(FRANCE)

Monteverde
COSTA RICA

Los Llanos
VENEZUELA

PACIFIC

OCEAN

ATLANTIC OCEAN

TROPIC OF CANCER

EQUATOR

SOUTH

AMERICA

Lake
Titicaca
BOLIVIA
and PERU

Atacama Desert
CHILE

TROPIC OF CAPRICORN

A F

| 0 | miles | 2000 |
| 0 | kilometers | 3000 |

OCEAN

EUROPE

ASIA

AFRICA

Nikkō
JAPAN

Genkai
JAPAN

TROPIC OF CANCER

Kathmandu
NEPAL

Jaisalmer
INDIA

PACIFIC

OCEAN

EQUATOR

INDIAN

OCEAN

MAURITIUS

Hinchinbrook
AUSTRALIA

Taveuni
FIJI

TROPIC OF CAPRICORN

AUSTRALIA

The World's Secret Places

● Islands   ▲ Mountains and Deserts   ☐ Pastoral Enclaves

*Positions are plotted at geographic
center of each feature.*

A séga dancer from Mauritius twirls on the beach.

Introduction

Two roads diverged in a wood, and I—I took the one less traveled by,
And that has made all the difference.

I BLAME THAT ENTICING FRAGMENT by Robert Frost for my years of world-wandering. I've always tended to take things too literally, and Frost's lines released my hidden world-wanderer—a character that had been dormant too long. Although I was born in Yorkshire, it was in America that I began turning off the main highways onto less traveled byways. I quickly learned to take the shunpike at every opportunity, measuring my way by the sun and the shadow lines, letting serendipity shape my experiences.

Soon I was hooked. Backroading had become an addiction. Today, I still have trouble resisting dirt tracks, country lanes, and forest roads. During these journeys, I have found deep and undisturbed woods, vales, and hollows bathed in sparkling mists, mountain ridges like eagle aeries, and deserts enticingly infinite.

But—as I sensed it would—the urge set in to explore places other than in America. I sought even more extravagant adventures in places far less familiar, with people whose words I could not understand but whose hearts and spirits seemed to speak clearly. Intent on becoming an Earth gypsy, I embraced the beautiful blue ball that is our Earth and roamed through its cultures, hidden corners, and lost worlds. On almost every continent, I visited secluded islands, high mountain regions, vast deserts, and pastoral enclaves so far off the tourist track, and so untainted by conflict or commercialism, that they qualify for me as "secret places."

I searched for these idyllic hideaways because my quieter self longed to leave the throngs behind, to seek out undiscovered nooks and crannies. My soul and spirit cried for—well—just what I hope I've provided in this *National Geographic Guide to The World's Secret Places*. I've discovered places away from the tumult and tension of crowds, which I'd like to share with you. Places that can be appreciated peacefully without the constriction of schedule-bound itineraries. Places that open us up to new ideas, new insights, new oases of calm, and, who knows, maybe even new selves within our more familiar everyday self. Perhaps, this is a self that has never yet had the chance or the stimuli to emerge into full, fresh consciousness. Indeed, this is the permanent, enduring gift of travel. This is the bring-home bonanza that continues to enrich us long after the vivid immediacies of our adventures have faded. Thankfully, our world still remains a thing of enormous mystery, silence, and secrets. Just as we are—to ourselves.

Islands

Breaking waves echo in evening light on Fiji.

Canada

GRAND MANAN

Scene: A dark, thundery day on Grand Manan, which is celebrated as "The Queen of the Fundy Isles."

ON THE horizon, a ball of black cumulus sits directly over an island, a strong and lonely place. Shafts of sun turn its rocky bulk into patch-works of bright greens and bronzes. Cliffs rise hundreds of feet from the surf to fir-topped crags. No houses, no smoke, no boats, none of the dainty accoutrements of islands farther to the south—just spectacular basaltic cliffs, forests full of life, unpredictable clouds, and the ocean. A true haven for secret-places collectors.

The island of Grand Manan is a 55-square-mile southern outpost of Canada, accessible only from the Canadian side of the notorious Bay of Fundy. While claiming the bay for France in 1604, an alarmed Samuel de Champlain recorded in his log that rivers in this odd place surged like tidal waves back up their channels every high tide "as if the Earth had hastily tipped."

With tidal variations as high as 40 feet, one can appreciate his anxiety. In fact, authorities claim that each tidal surge is equal to the aver-age 24-hour flow of all rivers in the world—more than 100 billion tons of water pouring in and out every 12 hours, 25 minutes. Despite numer-ous elaborate schemes for harnessing this water-power, the bay remains impressively untamed.

Grand Manan, celebrated as "The Queen of the Fundy Isles," has a strong, self-possessed feel to it—the kind of place you know you have to explore in spite of erratic ferries, summer blackflies, few beaches, and virtually no diver-sions except those found in the company of individuals who share a mutual love of remote, undiscovered places. I came here hoping to free myself from the spirit-strangling tyranny of schedules and prepackaged expectations, and the island cooperated. Bountifully.

AMONG THE first settlers here in 1784 were Loyalists from the United States, who had been run out of East Coast cities following the Dec-laration of Independence. Later residents included writer Willa Cather and her compan-ion Edith Lewis. The pair spent many summers on this cliff-bound bastion of basalt in a cot-tage hidden behind trees overlooking Whale Cove. Lewis described the place as "tranquiliz-ing to the spirit, opening up great spaces for it to roam in." Cather found the island inspiringly simple and primitive, "a quiet resource, a con-genial place to write in that beautiful silence, with the wind blowing in the elder bushes and the songs of hundreds of birds."

Basalt cliffs rise above exposed beaches on Grand Manan.

I felt the change of pace as soon as I arrived, after a calm two-hour, 20-mile crossing from Blacks Harbour, near St. George, in New Brunswick. Within minutes I was a welcome guest at the Compass Rose, a tiny shore-side hotel in North Head village with cozy bedrooms, a small dining room full of fresh flowers, and a terrace overlooking the harbor.

Soon lunch was served: A bowl of fresh fish chowder brimming with cream and presented with a small home-baked whole-wheat loaf, followed by coquilles St. Jacques—a generous helping of melt-in-the-mouth scallops basking in a rich, creamy sauce, accompanied by a salad flecked with dulse, Grand Manan's famous edible seaweed.

Looking south from the terrace across Long Island Bay's spindly fishing weirs, with such defeatist names as No Good, Try Again, and Hard Luck, I could see swaths of dark-green fir forests covering much of the island. From the eastern shoreline, cut with coves and protected by a scattering of tiny islets, Grand Manan tilts upward toward the 400-foot basalt cliffs of its western edge, rising like battlements from the ocean. What paved roads there are along the 18-mile-long eastern shore follow from the small lighthouse at North Head. A rough road cuts a four-mile link across the island to the sandbar-protected cove of Dark Harbour, the center of the island's periwinkle gathering and dulse harvesting.

A purse seiner at dock awaits the mending of torn nets.

To some, Dark Harbour is known as the dulse capital of the world. Here a handful of fishermen spend the summer months dragging thick ribbons of purple seaweed ashore at low tide to drying nets set up along the rocky beach. This drying process cannot be rushed, though; much of the fishermen's time is passed paying social six-pack calls among the lopsided tar paper cabins above the high-tide mark. Usually before sunset the mats of dulse are rolled and loaded into trucks, then transported to a processing facility where the dulse is either ground into powder for medicines and flavorings or packaged, whole and unprocessed, as an edible snack, aptly described as "seaweed jerky."

"It's a nice, quiet kinda life," a fisherman told me. He was looking out over Seal Cove and mending an 800-foot-long weir. "Dulsin' gives us somethin' to do when the herring's not runnin'."

During one of my earlier visits here, I had met Gleason Green, "85 years young" and living by himself in a house close to his fishing sheds on the bay. Green was a lobsterman, boat-builder, craftsman, green-thumb gardener, passable cook, inventor, raconteur, and enthusiastic world traveler. Mostly, though, he was a local resident worried about the absence of herring in the sea. Smoked herring is perhaps the oldest traditional product of the island. It not only is a source of income for fishermen and their families, but also provides a terrific food source that can last multiple days without refrigeration.

"There was a time boats'd come back after haulin' and they'd be full of herrin'," Green recalled. "Tumblin' over the side they'd be, enough to keep a hundred smokehouses on the

Fishing weir nets glow in the setting sun near Grand Manan.

go." For unknown reasons, the herring have since become elusive, leaving island fishermen reliant on lobsters and scallops.

"Lobsters are fine, though. More than enough for everybody. You can make a good livin' here off lobsters and scallops. I've still got the record: When I was 76, I brought the biggest catch ever come into this island in one day—3,600 pounds. I hauled a little under 300 traps and sold 'em at $3.30 a pound. Figure that out for a day's work."

THE BEST place to begin your own island exploration is at Southwest Head, where the road is a dusty dirt track winding through forest. A footpath leads up past the lighthouse to the cliff edge, where thousands of broken basalt columns rise like organ pipes from the surf hundreds of feet below.

Hiking is taken seriously on the island: More than 18 signed and well-maintained footpaths offer more than 50 miles of "the best darned walks in New Brunswick," as one enthusiast put it. To the east are dozens of islets—some mere rocky outcrops, others more substantial such as uninhabited Ross Island, accessible on foot at low tide, and White Head Island, reached by a free ferry from Ingalls Head.

Highlights of a drive along the bays and coves of the eastern shore are the picturesque groupings of shacks, herring smokehouses, and old canneries at North Head, Woodwards Cove, and Seal Cove. If you have the remotest urge to paint or take photographs, you'll come to know the latter well: At Seal Cove you can spend hours exploring the warped wharves, weather-worn warehouses, and narrow alleys smelling of lobsters and tar, all watched over by two churches on the hillside above.

Religion is no casual matter here. With 15 churches serving the island's resident population of 2,500, most recreational and social activities are church related. As one elderly lady told me, "Everyone knows what you're doing any time day or night. You either live celibate or you soon get a reputation."

IF YOU want to visit the outer islands—particularly Kent Island and Machias Seal Island, with their colonies of rare arctic terns, razorbills, petrels, puffins, and auks—plenty of boatmen are usually around to help, or the hotels will arrange transport. If you feel more adventurous, go fishing or lobstering with an island fisherman. Better yet, join one of the whale-watching trips offered by a number of agencies and also by the Marathon Inn, a mansarded masterpiece of Victorian architecture that perches high on the hillside overlooking North Head's harbor. The inn is a short stroll from the Whale and Sea Bird Research Station, a rich repository of whale lore and island history.

The Grand Manan Museum in Grand Harbour village offers an eclectic collection of 300 stuffed island birds, interesting marine and geology displays, archives of genealogies and documents relating to the island's history, a few of Willa Cather's treasured trinkets, and some sketches by John James Audubon. In 1831, Audubon became the first to document Grand Manan's amazing variety of bird life. Avid local ornithologist Allan Moses, who lived from 1881-1953 and was known as the "Island Bird Man," spent a lifetime assembling this remarkable display.

Best of all, on warm summer days, are the secluded beaches at—Red Point, with unusual rock formations and "magnetic" sand; Castalia, a favorite with residents; and Whale Cove.

I spent a quiet afternoon at Whale Cove toward the end of my stay. A few dulsers were around, sipping beer and nonchalantly exchanging nuggets of local gossip. Behind me, peering through the trees, was the cottage where Willa Cather had spent her summers writing novels. I felt inspired, just as she had. I took a deep breath, relaxed, and felt my spirit soar. There were so many great spaces for it to roam in.

TRAVEL NOTES

CLIMATE: Summer temperatures are warm with cool nights. Fog often rolls in, but burns off later in the day. Winters can bring snow or freezing rain.

EASE OF ACCESS: Daily ferry trips from Blacks Harbour, New Brunswick. Once there, cars, taxis, bicycles, or a good pair of hiking boots can be used.

HIGHLIGHTS: Bird-watching (more than 300 species live here or pass by), whale-watching, hiking, lolling on beaches, and gorging on seafood. The farmers market sells crafts, fresh foods, and smoked fish every Saturday from June through September.

United States

VINALHAVEN

Here live descendants of quarrymen, cutters of the island's gray-blue granite, used to build the Brooklyn Bridge.

"IT'S BLOWIN' a tad of a gale out there—it's gonna be a roller so watch out for a touch of the williwaws!" warns Captain Ray O'Neal with a wry smile. And indeed he's right. The one-and-a-quarter-hour trip from the tough little port-cum-artists' community of Rockland, Maine, begins boisterously as the *Governor Curtis* passenger and vehicle ferry hits open water beyond Owl's Head. A brief period of ocean swells brings passengers to the rail, greened. They hang there, leaning toward the rocking waters beneath a bruised and shredded sky.

One passenger tells me that on "thick o'fog" windless days, the area can become a strange silvered world of mist and silence. The driver of a lopsided truck, piled high with full propane tanks for the islanders' homes, wobbles with the heaving boat and looks warily at the tank ropes and wheel chocks. "Ah, I think she's gonna be okay," he bawls against the furious wind to his co-driver. His companion says nothing, but seems to be slowly backing away. "You think—ah'l hope" he mutters.

Finally, within the lee of eight-by-six-mile Vinalhaven Island, the sea calms and the boat passes snuggling coves and smooth granite ledges topped by deep, amazingly dark forests.

Strong images of a sturdy land are increasing. A wooden shack peeps out from the gloom. An upturned schooner painted brown and cream makes a cozy home for some loner; smoke eases out through a lopsided metal chimney. A couple of kids by the ferry rail in thick parkas wave, but nobody waves back.

Boats and lobster "cars" bob daintily near the piers of Carver's Harbor, and a scattering of white homes, cubist-patterned fish houses, and church towers come together in a huddle of stores and Victorian mansions along Main Street, below lushly wooded Armbrust Hill.

I leave the ferry with relief and stroll down the street to sketch a particularly bulky, 1885 dowager-duchess structure, laced with Carpenter-Gothic finery, known as the Star of Hope. It is owned, and has been restored, by renowned artist Robert Indiana.

"He was at it f'over 15 years," grumbles an elderly lady resident who happens to be passing by. "Off island too much he was. They say he's a very fast painter n'all, but you wouldn't know it from his work here!...Ayuh, gets me real exercised and spleeny. Honest it does."

Vinalhaven, one of the largest island communities along Maine's coast, is synonymous

Just off Vinalhaven Island, sailors take advantage of coastal winds.

with granite. Scores of the East Coast's most prominent structures, including the Brooklyn Bridge, parts of the Washington Monument, and railroad stations in Philadelphia and Chicago, are sheathed in the island's gray-blue and gray-pink rock, which quarrymen cut from Vinalhaven's bedrock before World War II, when the quarries closed. A large, majestic carving of an eagle intended originally for one of these edifices, and a scattering of finely polished fountains around town are reminders of the island's heritage. Up the hill from Main Street, on the village green beside a bandstand still used for regular concerts, is an enormous bright-blue galamander. The contraption, with 10-foot-high rear wheels, was the main form of horse- or ox-drawn transportation for moving granite blocks, up to a hundred tons each, from the quarry to the wharf and onto the huge "stone sloops" that carried the blocks by sea to the burgeoning East Coast cities.

Fresh lobster

The granite era has long ended and lobsters are what the island is all about today. More than 200 licensed lobstermen go out hauling from Carver's and Robert's Harbors; the new square-type lobster pots (far less romantic than the old domed ones) are piled up by the hundreds most everywhere you look around the docks.

"It's a pretty profitable business," says Elaine Crossman, co-owner with her husband, Phil, of Tidewater Motel overlooking Carver's Harbor.

"Y'see this is still a real working island— great place for adventure travelers, but not so hot for your average tourist—all your 'summer complaints,' 'coneheads' (tourists who love ice cream), 'rusticators,' 'flatlanders,' and 'from away' people. We got lots a' great names for 'em! But if you're up to adventure, it's a beautiful place. Great hikes. Miles of trails and little nature preserves, thanks to our Vinalhaven Land Trust office. A lot of our 10,000-acre island is protected land. They keep things right. We don't have fancy bistros here, and most places close up pretty early 'cept maybe for Candlepin Lodge out in the woods over there. If you like pool, candlepin bowling, a dinnah of chowdah, fried dough, lobster rolls, and lots a' 'go-withs,' you'll love that place. Wicked good!"

DESCENDANTS OF original late-18th-century settler-families— the Calderwoods, Coombs, Carvers, and Dyers—still comprise the majority of the island's 1,100 or so residents. The late Ivan Calderwood captured the traditional flavor of the island in his delightful series, the Uncle Dave books, which reflects "the days of fellowship in Uncle Dave's fish house for old salts." Harold Vinal's poetry reflects the mysterious beauty of these "misty, emerald-fingered islands." Residents love their books and their weekly newsletter, The Wind. The elegantly columned Carnegie Library on the green by the bandstand, across from the summer Saturday flea market, is always a popular meeting place. The librarian, looking demure and bookish, whispers surreptitiously as we sit closely together at her desk.

"You wouldn't believe the things I hear about the islanders. I'm from away, so it's like I'm not really here when they get started. I tell you, it's wilder than any TV soap opera! But people have good hearts, too. We all work together without really thinking about it. That's one of the best things about living on an island. You look out for each other."

FARTHER DOWN Main Street, the breeze blows an aroma of fish chowder, fried haddock, and lobster rolls from an array of small eateries. There I discovered a prototypical New England scene: Rockwellian huddles of elderly gentlemen, obviously retired lobstermen, sip their coffees and exchange "I remember when" tales, oblivious to the intrusions of hungry visitors. I try to listen in, but all I get is a mishmash of dialectal obscurities full of complaints about arthritis and odd lobstering references to shedders, selects, snappers, soft-shells, culls, molts, hods, pots, cars, pounds, and no-good sternmen! I sense a tenacious clinging to old secrets.

On East Main, edged by deep woods, is a perfect swimming hole at Booth's Quarry. On a sticky summer day, there's no finer pastime than a plunge into the dark cold waters and a lay back on cool rock, watching the clouds pass, dainty as duck down.

The days move slowly here. The pace of Vinalhaven encourages long walks along shady forest trails opening suddenly onto coves and bright white sand beaches—ideal for periods of mellow introspection. Those who choose to stay awhile on Vinalhaven enjoy a far wider selection of hiking options. Just behind the community medical center, for example, is the lovely Armbrust Hill Town Park, a 30-acre delight of landscaped walks among old quarries. One of

the island's late residents, the beloved Betty Roberts, invested years of hard work and creativity to make this little masterpiece, a haven of peace for residents and visitors alike.

One of my favorite walks, particularly around sunrise, is to Arey's Neck Woods, which surrounds the rocky Geary's Beach on the eastern edge of the island. You can sit here, in the lee of a fallen tree, and listen to the hush and rustle of dawn while watching the emerging cracks of color spread across the still sea. Often my restless nature prefers action to silence, but the island taught me other ways. Geary's Beach gave me one of those treasured experiences when time seems unimportant and thoughts meld into the gently lapping ocean and the easing of dawn breezes.

The elemental grace of this Maine island keeps coming back in faint memories that vanish like the end of a dream. I find myself agreeing with John Fowles's description of the special magic that islands can possess: "They strip and dissolve the crud of our pretensions and cultural accretions. One returns to the roots of something beyond one's personal descent."

TRAVEL NOTES

CLIMATE: For swimming, June through September has the best temperatures. Chilly climate between November and April. **EASE OF ACCESS:** A one-hour ferry ride from Rockland; on the island, hiking and biking are the best ways to explore. Many unpaved roads. **HIGHLIGHTS:** Small seafood restaurants and cafés. Some lovely secret places maintained by the Vinalhaven Land Trust.

Sloops, schooners, and barges travel Vinalhaven's main road — the Atlantic Ocean.

Guadeloupe
ÎLES DES SAINTES

Most visitors come for the day.
Secret-place seekers, however,
will wish they could stay for years.

A VISIT to Guadeloupe's islands will be a truly serendipitous experience, the kind you've always promised yourself—where you can wander lazily among tiny islands barely visible on most maps, abandon rigid itineraries, discard timepieces, feel the days flow seamlessly, and let a journey take on its own rhythm and pace.

Hardly an hour south by ferry from Guadeloupe's biggest city, Pointe-à-Pitre, among the eight-island archipelago of Les Saintes, which has ancient volcanic cones, cliffs, and coves, is the islet of Terre-de-Haut. Here the perfumed breezes of dusk ease down the scrub- and forest-covered hills surrounding the harbor at Le Bourg, the only town on this two-by-three-mile islet, population barely 1,500.

I'm sitting on a bench in the harbor square by the gilded column commemorating the centennial of the French Revolution and encrusted with those ringing words—Liberté! Égalité! Fraternité! The people here are proud of their French heritage, derived from Breton and Norman sailors and settlers. I catch fragments of soft conversation in French-Creole patois from the shadowy stoops. (Basic French will get you by here, but learning a few Creole expressions helps.)

A young girl with honey-colored skin scampers by, her bare feet slapping on the street still moist from an evening sprinkling of rain, her long blonde cornsilk hair streaming. The glow of the day's heat still radiates off the wood and stucco walls of this clustered community of red roofs, brightly painted shutters, and fragments of gingerbread trim. The last of the sunlight bathes the palm fronds, mango and breadfruit trees, the yuccas, and the flamboyants (or flame trees). The town is settling into a whispery evening.

I can hear the chink of glasses and the muted back-beat of zouk music from the harborside restaurants melding with the slow lappings of lethargic waves and the chitter of sand grains in the undertow. One hill has a striking sugarloaf character so, inevitably, it has been named Pain de Sucre. To me the intense, sparkling light, the gorgeous multihued blues of the ocean, and the scattering of white-walled, scarlet-roofed houses make it appear pure French Mediterranean.

ÎLES DES SAINTES, also known as Les Saintes, may appear as insignificant blips in the great arc of Caribbean islands, yet the bold remnants

Tropical breezes sway palm fronds that frame a Caribbean bay.

of French fortifications overlooking Le Bourg reflect a long and rigorous history of strategic skirmishes and major naval battles between the French and British. What better place, then, to begin explorations of this tiny island than on the breezy crags north of town, strolling the meticulously laid basalt walls of Fort Napoléon. Completed in the mid-19th century, the fort replaced one built in the 17th. Today this splendidly restored example of military architecture is the showpiece of this "Gibraltar of the Antilles."

The French finally defeated the British in 1816 without ever firing a shot from the Fort

Napoléon ramparts. Elegant cactus gardens have long since replaced the batteries, and the barracks now house a museum of island history and life, as well as a modest gallery of modern art lively in graphic style but somewhat indifferent in quality.

Terre-de-Haut's highest point, to the southwest, is the burly 1,014-foot summit of Le Chameau, topped by a sturdy stone defense tower. I climbed the rusty vertical ladder to the battlements and could see the islets of Les Saintes and, to the north, Guadeloupe's two islands: Basse-Terre, with its cloud-clad active volcano, Soufrière; and Grande Terre. To the

Trade winds gust during the last hours of daylight.

east were the hazy outlines of La Désirade and Marie-Galante. Eleven islands in a single sweep.

I could also see near Îlet à Cabrit the blue and orange fishing boats, called *saintoises*—mainstay of Terre-de-Haut's economy. These graceful 20-foot-long crafts, powered by outboard motors, are considered to be some of the best built traditional boats in the Caribbean. In addition to their daily harvestings of conch, lobster, crayfish, sea urchins, red snapper, carangue, and coffre, the fishermen here enjoy a reputation for their courage and ability to net enormous winter catches of tuna, kingfish, and dorade. Samples can be enjoyed smoked, grilled, poached in court bouillon or marinated *à la Tahitienne* in the island's excellent—if occasionally expensive—restaurants.

As I strolled the soft sand beaches, I noticed piles of *filets bleus*, blue nets strung with orange buoys. I watched fishermen meticulously mending these intricate webs and making new ones in the shade of their small harborside homes. A few people still wore the traditional island *salako*—a cloth-covered variant of the broad-brimmed coolie hat used by Indo-Chinese laborers who came to work in the islands following the abolition of slavery here in 1848.

I chatted with Bernard Boucage and his son as they constructed the sturdy superstructure for yet one more of their famed saintoise boats. "How long will it take to build?" I asked.

Bernard smiled, tipped his head at the beguiling angle of the RCA Victor dog, and replied with a typical islander's French shrug, followed by these words: "I build the best boats—so what does time matter?"

I followed his example and forgot time, too, wandering the island's narrow roads and rutted

At the local market tropical fruits entice buyers.

tracks on my hired scooter (there are only a handful of cars here), seeking secluded beaches with long expanses of untouched sand and soft ocean breezes carrying the musky smell of the sea. Each place I discovered was more enticing than the last. Anse Crawen at the western tip is supposed to be for nude bathers, but except for a couple of topless beauties, modesty prevailed here as I sunned myself on the warm, creamy sand.

At Anse du Figuier, I shared seclusion with bull-headed goats and cud-chewing cows. At the lovely arc of Petite Anse below Terre-de-Haut's famed Pain de Sucre, I swam in a perfect turquoise-blue bay before sampling the island's ti'punch, a pleasantly potent blend of

white rum, sugar syrup, and lime, at a nearby modest hotel. This combination is the ideal antidote to crotch-pounding scooter-rides along the rough, unpaved roads of the island.

I finally found my perfect beach early one morning, before the day-trippers from Guadeloupe arrived, at Anse de Pompièrre. I sat among swaying palms looking out across a hill-bound bay at the eroded crags and pinnacles of Roches Percées, where pirates are said to have buried their ill-gotten bounty.

The idea of hidden treasure intrigued me, but more satisfying were the island's tangible treasures, particularly its Creole-inspired seafood cuisine, prepared with French meticulousness by Terre-de-Haut's renowned female chefs. This little place is a gastronomic paradise and eating a social art—from the morning snap of crusty warm baguettes and the buttery richness of fresh croissants, to lunches of *accras* (fish fritters), stuffed *christophene* (squash), *blaff de poisson* (poached fish in a rich broth), *crabes farcis* (aromatic stuffed land crabs), delicate pâté-like *boudin de poisson* (fish sausage), and a more aromatic blood sausage known as *boudin Creole*.

Then comes a welcome pause—the afternoon siesta when shops close, scooters cease their prattle (by law!), and fishermen sleep off rum-laced repasts—before it all begins again with dinner, usually served between seven and nine. An early night is usually essential here—if only to restore metabolisms in time for those first baguettes of morning.

WHILE I had come too late for the island's grand Saintes Festival of August 15 and 16 (the first day celebrates an early defeat of the British in 1666; the second commemorates the Virgin Mary and sailors lost at sea), I found I needed no organized distractions here. True, I would have loved to watch the Feast of All Saints rituals on November 1, when the cemetery, just over a hill behind Le Bourg, becomes a candlelit wonderland, but it's the little images of everyday life that persist—the pleasurable frissons from memories of island life in the Lesser Antilles.

I remember watching the pterodactyl-like frigate birds circling the hills with motionless wings before plunging to snatch a snack of flying fish from the harbor; the smile in the eyes of sculptor Hoff Jerame as he sold me one of his palm branches painted with a demon's face; and the grin of "Bon-Bon" Humbert, a beloved old island fisherman who's always at the harbor wearing his salako hat. Also memorable are the sudden *thwack* of heat and humidity as the early sun rises above the old volcanoes; the rapturous morning cooing of doves and the frantic antics of tiny yellow-breasted sucrier birds trying to sneak grains of sugar from my breakfast table; the bleat of goats on the cactus and scrub-covered cliffs above the secluded beaches; the simple church near the park, illuminated at night by strings of golden lights; the palm-frond-and-bamboo funkiness of the disco down by the cemetery; and the utter silence of a moonlit midnight swim with the day's heat still vibrant in the water.

Terre-de-Haut exudes pure spirit of place. This tiny island envelopes you in its unique magic. Devoid of excessive tourist trappings, it remains true to itself, simple yet quietly sophisticated, a haven for travelers who relish the joys of solitude and lazy days of gauzy insights and subtle sensory delights. It's a place you carry with you—a place that truly asks, "So what does time matter?"

TRAVEL NOTES

CLIMATE: February to April are dry months; July to November are wet. Summers reach 90°F. Avoid the busy season, near the New Year. **EASE OF ACCESS:** Daily flights leave from Pointe-à-Pitre; daily ferries from Pointe-à-Pitre and Trois Rivières. **HIGHLIGHTS:** Windsurfing and fishing, although currents can be strong. Scuba diving and snorkeling. French and Creole architecture, cuisine, and a laissez-faire mood. Colonial history. Biking, strolling, beach-lounging, snorkeling, bird-watching, and dining.

Scotland

HARRIS

This wild island offers few luxuries,
yet possesses white beaches, Gaelic culture,
and world-renowned Harris tweed.

THAT OLD Hebridean saying is correct—the rain does come down horizontally on the wild Scottish island of Harris, and it was indeed a "warm rain" that greeted me when I arrived here for the first time in June. It was also angled in its wild descent, both sharp and violent. The winds shrieked like banshees across the brown-gray wilderness of dead heather and lichen-covered boulders. The normally still, almost sinister surfaces of the black lochans among the bogs were whipped into froth by the gale; the brittle marsh grasses lay broken by the downpour in the glowering bleakness below the eroded edges of ancient peat banks.

I was atop Clisham—or, as they say in the Gaelic that is commonly spoken here, Na Hearadh—on Harris. At 2,619 feet, this is the highest peak in the Western Isles, and all around was a primeval scene of dark immensity—no signs of habitation anywhere, no welcoming curls of smoke, no walls, no trees, no patches of moorland flora among the eroded stumps of gneiss breaking through the peat like old bones on an almost fleshless torso. Here, overlooking the wild moorland moonscapes of this small Atlantic island, about 25 miles northwest of the Island of Skye, I sought shelter from the

storm—and found it among Europe's oldest rocks. Formed more than three billion years ago, gouged and rounded in three ice ages and sturdy enough to withstand three more, this part of our planet suggests Earth's earliest form. Another Hebridean saying seems to capture this, I think, when it claims that "when God made time, he made plenty of it." On the desolate slopes of Clisham, you do indeed feel time in its infinitely slow passage.

As I hid from the torrent, the clouds passed on, abruptly whirling eastward over The Little Minch sound toward the dagger-tipped black peaks of Skye. Suddenly the sun was warm again in a sparkling blue sky. Looking far below Clisham's western slope, I could see a scene that would seduce the most ardent admirers of far more tropical islands—great enticing arcs of creamy sand. Harris's west coast boasts some of the finest beaches in the archipelago: Lusken-tyre, Scarista, and Seilebost, fringed by high dunes and a turquoise ocean gently deepening to dark blue, lazily lapping on a shoreline unmarked by footprints for mile after mile.

For years I'd been promising myself a journey to Harris, this mysterious island where Scottish crofters still weave the world-famous

A storm lull on Harris inspires a walk through the heather.

Rugged seascapes mark the eastern shore of Harris.

Harris tweed—the clomor, or great cloth—in their own homes. Here in the Western Isles, or Outer Hebrides, "there are over 200 different islands," a pub owner in Ullapool had told me before I caught the ferry from the mainland. "And there was a time, not so very long ago, when every one of them had its crofters and its own kirks. But then came the terrible famines and all those great 'clearances' in the middle of the 19th century, when the big lairds got together, kicked many of the people off the land—sent them to Canada's Nova Scotia (New Scotland) and suchlike places—and moved the sheep in. Now I think

there are only 13 islands—maybe less—with any people left on them. Crofting's a hard life. You're a bit of everything—farmer, fisherman, peat gatherer, seaweed harvester, tweed weaver—you name it. And once in a wee while maybe even whisky maker too!"

The frisky three-hour ferry ride brought me, a little shaken, to Stornoway, capital of the Outer Hebrides chain. This charming little town of 8,600 people, the hub of life on the main island of Lewis, has one of the two airports in the Hebrides (the other is on Barra). After the slow seagoing route I had chosen, though, I was

in no mood for dallying and was soon driving south for 35 miles on the A859, over the bleak moors and peat bogs and across the narrow land bridge near Tarbert into Harris South.

I drove slowly alongside the thin strips of crofting land fringing the fertile meadows beside the coastal dunes and beaches. They say the milk of cows that graze here in the spring and summer is scented by the land's abundance of wildflowers—primroses, sea spurrey, campion, milkwort, sea pink, sorrel, and centaury. Each crofter's strip, or "lazy bed," usually no more than four acres in all, once had its own cottage (*tigh dubh*, or black house) set close to the narrow roads that wind around boulders and burns. A few tigh dubh remnants

had walls of crudely shaped bedrock, four feet thick in places. Some still had a roof of thick thatch made from barley stalks, which was held in place by a grid of ropes weighted down with large rocks. The windows were set deep in the walls, and the door openings were supported by lintel stones often over three feet thick. Most families on Harris now live in more recently built homes. The familiar dark brown piles of peat (*cruachs*), enough to heat a house for a whole year, are stacked along the outer walls.

Until the early and mid-1900s, these tigh dubh formed the communal living space for families and their livestock. I felt pulled back in time to the prehistoric origins of island life, long before the invasions of the Icelandic tribes

Changing winds dishevel matching clothes.

and the Norsemen from Scandinavia in the ninth century, long before the emergence of the Gaelic-speaking clans of the MacLeods, the MacAulays, and the MacRaes. All around the Outer Hebrides are ravaged remnants—strange totemic presences—of ancient cultures in the form of Stone Age brochs (lookout towers), Bronze Age burial mounds, and stone circles. The famous standing stones of Callandish on Lewis, 30 miles north of Tarbert, are thought to have been a key religious and astronomical focal point for island tribes since 3000 B.C.

I asked the postmistress at Scarista village about the famous Harris-tweed makers. "Och, you won't find so many now," she told me, "making it the old way in their own homes on their Hattersley looms. But you can usually hear the shuttles clickety-clacking way back up the roads."

She was right, for that is how I found Marion Campbell. She was one of Harris's most renowned weavers, at that time living in the tiny village of Plocrapool on the wild eastern side of the island known as Na Baigh (Bays). Through a dusty window of a weaving shed, I had seen an elderly woman with white hair working at an enormous wooden contraption. "Aye, come in now. Don't mind the smell. You can always tell a real Harris tweed," Marion told me. "There's always a bit of the peat-reek about it."

She worked her loom at an alarming pace, and the shed shook as she whipped the shuttle backward and forward between the warp yarns with bobbins of blue weft. I looked down and saw buckets brimming with bits of vegetation the color of dead skin. "That's crotal—lichen from the rocks. For my dyes."

In the days before chemical dyes, most spinners and weavers made their own from moorland plants and flowers—heather, bracken, irises, ragwort, marigolds—whatever was available. I pointed to a pile of tan-colored fleece and asked if it had been dyed with the lichen. Marion giggled. "Ooh—no, no, that's the peat, the peat soot. Makes a lovely shade." It also produces a cloth that looks like the land here.

On Harris you use what's at hand. In the last century there were well-intentioned but often eccentric schemes to "improve" this lonely island suffering from signs of terminal decline. One German inventor, Gerhard Zucher, failed gloriously, with an epic explosion, to promote "mail by rocket" as a way of speeding up the delivery of goods between the islands. The soap industry magnate, Lord Leverhulme, who purchased most of Harris in the early 1900s, tried to establish a major port at Leverburgh (it flopped), to make sausages for African nations from surplus whale meat (ditto), and even built an elaborate mill to increase the efficiency of the tweed industry (likewise ditto). Lady Dunmore, whose family built the grandiose baronial Amhuinnsuidhe Castle here in 1868, was more successful in her efforts to enhance the tweed industry by organizing the cottage-based system.

The main town of Tarbert (Tairbart in Gaelic), with a population of 500 huddled in fishing cottages around a small quay, is hardly anyone's idea of a Hebridean hot spot. The community of Rodel (Roghadal) possesses a sturdy 16th-century church with ornately carved tombs of the MacLeod chieftains, and there are a couple of notable hostelries on the island such as Scarista House and Ardhasaig House. You might catch glimpses of red deer, otters, golden eagles, and even the occasional dolphin off Bays. But none of these are the true appeal of this place. So what is the lure? Try silence, wilderness, solitude, and a soul-nurturing sense of coming home to something bold, basic, and honest.

In the end it's the islanders' endurance and traditional crofting and weaving ways that maintain the unique character of Harris. After all, there's not much diversion here unless you're a beachcomber; a driver in search of challenging roadmanship on one-lane roads; a lover of the traditional folksongs and tales offered at one of the community (alas rare) *ceilidh* sessions; or a determined hiker.

But most of all, it is that Hebridean light sparkling off those turquoise bays, and making all the colors—bronzes, ochers, mauves, pale and dark greens, and muted rusts—vibrant and luminous. Making Harris always as it promises to be: pure magic.

TRAVEL NOTES

CLIMATE: During the summer, it may stay light until 11 p.m. The only meteorological guarantee is that weather is always fickle. June through September is the prime season. **EASE OF ACCESS:** Flights from the British Isles to Stornoway in Lewis; ferry to Lewis from Ullapool. **HIGHLIGHTS:** Ancient island culture; Harris tweed; the 5,000-year-old Standing Stones of Callandish; crofter-farmers and weavers; hikes on the high, wild moors; a ceilidh evening of songs; and stories in an islander's home, or a local inn.

Portugal

SÃO MIGUEL

Floating in balmy, endless springtime warmth, São Miguel offers a glimpse of the legendary lost realm of Atlantis.

"OF COURSE this is Atlantis!" insisted eagle-featured Antonio Piñero, spitting his words out like olive pits. Most Azoreans have no doubts on the matter. We sat sipping coffee and *aguardente*—Azorean firewater made from the remnants of grape pressings—in an outdoor café overlooking the broad harbor at Ponta Delgada, capital of São Miguel. With a population of 22,000, it is the largest town in the 868-square-mile, nine-island archipelago of the Azores. Tony had been a modest, soft-spoken companion during my first hours in this little outpost of Portugal out in the North Atlantic Ocean, some 800 miles due west of Lisbon. But about this particular subject he tolerated no ambiguity whatsoever. From inside his worn wool jacket he pulled a much-thumbed book titled *Plato's History of Atlantis*.

"Was Plato a wise man?" Tony challenged, obviously preparing for a rhetorical foray. "Yes, he certainly was," he responded before I had a chance to say anything. "Now listen please to what he wrote." Tony turned the pages with solemnity. "'For in those days,'" he began, "'Atlantis was navigable from an island situated to the west of the straits, which you call

the Pillars of Hercules.'" He paused to interject, "That's Gibraltar—way out in the Mediterranean." Then he continued: "'The people despised everything but virtue, thinking lightly on the possession of gold and other property, which seemed a burden to them; neither were they intoxicated by luxury. Nor did they take up arms against one another.'"

Tony sighed. "We Azoreans are so like that. We are not very rich; we want only peace, a good honest life—and friends. Lots of good friends. And plenty of good wine!"

We ordered two more tiny cups of espresso with aguardente chasers. Sunshine sparkled across the harbor waves. Behind us, the white stucco and basalt tower of the Convent da Esperança rose from the ornately paved street. The whole plaza was surrounded by bright white stucco buildings with dark volcanic stone arches and windows. Shoeshine boys and women in thick shawls selling fruit milled around the arches by the church, setting up shop for the day. Strings of red lottery tickets, clipped up with old clothespins, dangled from rickety tables. The smell of freshly baked bread wafted downhill from the little hidden squares of the old town.

Rolling hills and sheer cliffs speak of São Miguel's volcanic origin.

A caldera glimmers among the trees.

"But what actually happened to Atlantis?" I asked.

"I will tell you," Tony said, searching the wrinkled pages of his book for the right quotation. "'But then there occurred violent earthquakes and floods and in a single day and night of rain all the men in a body sank into the earth, and the island of Atlantis in like manner disappeared beneath the sea. And there are remaining in small islets only the bones of the wasted body—the mere skeleton of the country being left.' And that," he added proudly, "is my country." We sat silently for quite a while.

Whether Atlantis or not, there is no doubt that the Azores have suffered earthquakes—not surprising since the islands lie at the restless junction of three tectonic plates. What is known for certain of the archipelago's history begins in 1427 (somewhat later than the old Atlantis legend), when navigators, sent by Portuguese prince Henry the Navigator noted the existence on their charts of some of the islands and claimed them for Portugal. Christopher Columbus stopped here briefly before, and after, discovering the New World. Further island discovery and colonization by both Portuguese and Flemish settlers continued slowly until the 16th and 17th centuries, when the Azores became important whaling islands and fulcrum points of trade between Europe and the newly emerging Americas. Portugal later gave the Azores status as an autonomous republic.

"So now you know!" Tony suddenly shouted in a flubberbastic outburst. "This is definitely Atlantis! If you don't believe me, I will show you how right Plato was in what he said. We go to Furnas. Now. Okay?"

We left the cobbled streets of Ponta Delgada behind and wound our way on narrow country roads up through green valleys and among goosebumpy hills, driving past cow-dotted fields bound by hedges of wild hydrangea. As we climbed up the volcanic spine of this 40-by-10-mile island, the homes of more than half the archipelago's population of 250,000 became more visible. Way down at the western end were shattered peaks and the great cone of Caldeira das Sete Cidades rising above a patchwork of fields and white-walled farmhouses and high-cliffed coves with black sand beaches.

"That's Furnas, over there." Tony pointed toward the tallest peaks. "When we arrive, I'll prove to you that Plato was right. But first—watch this hill and see what happens."

We were climbing steeply now on a road ablaze with more hydrangea hedgerows; a wind billowed across fields bright with hollyhocks, lilies, and dahlias. And then there was just space. We were suddenly floating in blue-sky limbo, among the clouds.

Tony laughed. "Now look," he said, and I realized we had driven up over the lip of a volcano. Three hundred feet directly below us lay the ancient crater, two miles wide and edged by eroded crags falling vertically into a royal-blue lake—the Lake of Fire (Lagoa do Fogo). The sight was mesmerizing. I felt I'd entered some secret place not intended for mortal eyes. Far below, a narrow peninsula, cloaked in remnants of a once vast primeval laurel forest, eased into the lake, a perfect white beach on its western

side. And we had the whole magical place to ourselves.

It was a moment I had no desire to end any time soon. Tony—this man with the tenacity of a pit bull and a heart of almost adolescent earnestness—had foreseen my mood. Out came a basket of lunchtime delights, including two snow-white rounds of queijo branco cheese, created from a centuries-old island recipe that combines cow's and goat's milk; big loaves of warm bread with deep golden crusts; a thick wedge of winy São Jorge cheese made on the nearby island of the same name and truly one of the world's classic cheeses; pungent slices of island-cured ham; a whole pineapple from one of São Miguel's greenhouse plantations; and two bottles of Portugal's sparkling vinho verde wine.

It was a long time before we moved on, and the mood of fantasy stayed with us.

Winding down the long slope from the crater, we passed tiny fields, vineyards, and orchards bounded by 20-foot-high beech hedges—protection against the winds that constantly buffet the islands. Nearby sat tall pyramidal frames on which corn was dried, and stationary solid-wheeled oxcarts with high wicker sides, still used for farm work. We drove past yam plantations crammed in junglelike valleys brimming with yellow and blue flowers, tobacco fields with tall slat-walled drying sheds, and even a tea plantation, established by two Chinese experts in 1878, bounded by hedges of araucarias and windbreaks of Japanese cedars.

"Every time you close your eyes, the island changes," Tony said. And he was right. So far I'd explored less than a third of São Miguel and already enjoyed fragments of Irish meadows, Scottish highlands, lush Indonesian jungles, alpine scenery with Japanese overtones,

The Atlantic Ocean Gulf Stream helps keep the Azores warm.

a volcanic moonscape, and a Chinese-inspired tea plantation in a Kashmir-foothills setting. All these exist in a humid, subtropical climate whose exposure to the Gulf Stream makes for perpetual springtime.

In the valley of Furnas, the magic became overwhelming. We had climbed over pine-shrouded volcanic hills and for a while were lost in mists, which cleared suddenly as we descended into the greenest of green valleys, dotted with white farms. The buildings of the stately town of Furnas—a popular spa for ailing Europeans in Victorian days—clustered around a series of rocky and noxious mini-craters: Some spewed blobs of boiling mud; others vented whirling steam and sulfurous geysers; still others emitted rushing, ice-cold spring water from cracks in the earth next to the hot jets.

Ponta Delgada Square

Tony led me down the stately main street right into Terra Nostra Park, where we lost ourselves in a fantastic profusion of tropical and fruit trees. A family sat picnicking by a warm lake fed by thermal springs. The picnickers were all dipping their feet and singing melancholy fado songs as the father played a 12-string guitar.

"Okay," Tony said, exuding an almost magisterial radiance. "A last bit of Plato. Please listen. 'Also, whatever fragrant things there are in the earth...all of these the sacred island lying beneath the sun brought forth fair and wondrous in infinite abundance.' "

The Azores, particularly the island of São Miguel, were once known as the "breadbasket of Portugal." They are still famous for the profusion of their fruits and flowers and for the three-harvests-a-year fecundity of their volcanic soils. They have a sizable beef-and-dairy industry, too. Nowhere else have I seen such natural abundance. Certainly no other Atlantic islands can match the Azores in this respect.

"Okay, Tony," I finally gave in. "I'm in Atlantis!" And I chuckled, amused by how certain we all sometimes pretend to be in our absolute sureness of nothing at all.

Tony then nodded, happy that Plato and he had once again been vindicated. "Good— now let's eat," he said.

I expected to dine in the restaurant at the Hotel Terra Nostra, a fascinating art deco masterpiece, but instead we joined a group of Tony's friends who were sprawled beside a rather large pile of freshly turned earth near Lake Furnas. Dinner, I gathered from the laying out of cloths and plates on the grass, was about to be served. But there was no sign of food. The wine flowed, followed by more local firewater brandy, plus São Miguel passion-fruit liqueur. And still no food!

Finally one of the men rose (somewhat unsteadily) and began flailing away at the pile of earth with a small shovel. Fragrant billows of hot steam poured from the ground. Then—to the enthusiastic applause of the group—he plunged his hand into the foot-deep hole and withdrew an enormous cloth sack. He passed the sack to his wife, who delicately unfolded the complex layerings to expose a wonderfully fragrant mélange of chicken pieces, sausages, yams, and garlic—a remarkable meal prepared volcano-style.

THE NEXT day I explored the far western end of the island, spiraling once again up the slopes of an ancient volcano to discover the beautiful Caldeira das Sete Cidades snuggled deep in the hollow of a rugged crater. I sat on the grassy rim and gazed down on the still, silent waters for a long, long time.

I think it was this silence that finally seduced me. I had made plans to visit the eight other Azorean islands spread across 400 miles of the Atlantic Ocean. But somehow the peace of São Miguel made me realize that to leapfrog from island to island in the short time I had would mean sacrificing the very things I had come to find—tranquility and the chance to understand a little about island life and ways in this isolated world-within-a-world. So—I stayed.

The balmy days passed slowly. I explored every nook and cranny of the island, meeting the old fishermen of Rabo de Peixe on the wave-lashed northern coast; sitting in with a group of islanders near Vila Franca do Campo to play Azorean folk songs on a confusing array of stringed instruments; exploring remnants of old lava flows; and visiting a secluded island home distillery, where an old man and his wife produced some of the finest fruit brandies I've ever tasted, using an ancient array of boiling pots, copper tubes, and cooling pans.

Somewhere along the way I met a scrimshander from the whaling village of Lajes do Pico, whose artistic etching of whale teeth had made him something of a national treasure. "There are more Azoreans in New England than the whole population of the islands today," he told me. "You can make good money in America, but..." he paused and looked around at the mountains, the myriad greens of the stone-walled fields, the little white villages, the vast expanse of blue ocean in all directions. "but...after a while you need to come home again. This is a very special place."

Some of the mainland Portuguese see these islands as rather backward, geologically unstable (there's always an expectation of yet one more earthquake or a new emerging volcano), economically stagnant, and lacking the sophistication of the motherland. Others, however, are wiser. They perceive, in these tiny, fertile fragments of earth and the peaceful ways of the people, ancient touchstones of enduring values and mutual integrity. Something, in fact, that reflects the very essence of Atlantis.

Plato would have been proud.

TRAVEL NOTES

CLIMATE: A perpetual springtime climate moderated by the Gulf Stream makes most months enjoyable times to visit. Winters can be wet and windy. **EASE OF ACCESS:** A car is best for enjoying the attractions on the island. Rental rates are comparable with those in the U.S. **HIGHLIGHTS:** Wild hydrangea and azalea. The Caldeira das Sete Cidades crater with its twin lakes, the Lagoa do Fogo, and the steaming hot springs and fumaroles of Furnas. The Nordeste region is one of the wildest areas, boasting the island's highest peak, Pico da Vara.

Spain
GOMERA

Ancient culture, secluded bays and beaches, and Garajonay National Park await those who learn of this forgotten isle.

GOMERA IS one of seven Canary Islands studding the sea 200 miles off the southwestern coast of Morocco. Pliny the Elder, a Roman natural historian and scientist, dubbed the Canaries the "Fortunate Isles" for their balmy, year-round sea breezes. The most popular of the Canary Islands are the two jet-setter destinations of Gran Canaria and Tenerife, followed by lava-black Lanzarote and Fuerteventura, with its strange desert-like beaches. The remaining three—the smaller, more remote islands of Hierro, La Palma, and Gomera—attract only a handful of travelers willing to sacrifice the sun, sand, and disco din of a large, all-inclusive island resort for the enchantments of a small, undiscovered island.

Of the forgotten three, Gomera is perhaps the most exotic. It's a round, 146-square-mile beauty with a resident population of about 12,000. Dominating the island is the 4,879-foot-high extinct volcanic cone of Garajonay; from its cloud-whipped summit, deeply furrowed ravines radiate like spokes in a wheel, often ending in towering basalt cliffs. On this remote island, dense, moist forests of laurel crowd the higher slopes in such unique lushness that in 1986 UNESCO declared almost 10,000 acres of the land a World Heritage site. Indeed, most of Gomera's rugged uplands are part of a giant greenhouse microenvironment in which 400 or so plant species that have been extinct in Europe and Africa for millions of years still flourish in the humidity perpetuated by springs, streams, and trade-wind mizzle (mist and drizzle).

Adding to Gomera's remote, exotic qualities are the languages of the island people. In addition to the spoken language that distinguishes all Canarios from mainland Spaniards, (a Spanish that drops letters, replaces consonants, slurs words, and displays distinct accents from one island to the next), on Gomera, there is also a language without words.

A remnant of the ancient pre-Christian Guanche culture, the timeless whistling language—el silbo, a shrill, staccato Morse code—is still used occasionally by shepherds to communicate with one another across the deep, pathless ravines. These eerie echoes, rebounding off the high volcanic cliffs, reinforce Gomera's reputation as a wild and primitive place. If you ever get to see a shepherd vaulting down a near-vertical

Garajonay National Park protects the lush laurel forests on Gomera.

hillside with his tall *astia* pole, or devouring a traditional meal of watercress soup, roasted rabbit, and ghastly green *gofio* (a mulch of roasted grains, corn, and water), you'll have glimpsed ancient practices that are part of the Guanches' enduring heritage.

TUMBLING FROM these ragged upper ravines, past meticulous emerald farming terraces that resemble Bali's renowned topography, are Gomera's unforgettable views—farmland speckled with tiny white cubist houses; hamlets broken by clusters of palm trees; banana fields; tiny walled plots of mangoes, guavas, and corn; and high, rugged cliffs; and black sand coves.

All roads on Gomera lead eventually to and from the port and capital of San Sebastián on the eastern side of the island, which looks rather North African: Colorful clusters of homes fill the narrow barrancos and climb the steep sides of dry canyon walls. Here 6,000 or so people live slow-paced lives. They saunter to cafés and bars around the harbor, sampling the tapas dishes of octopus, calamari, olives, and anchovies, or proudly pointing out the sights of the town to visitors. Most notable is the Church of Iglesia de la Virgen de la Asunción, in which, some claim, Columbus attended mass before his departure on September 6, 1492, for the New World. That is why some call Gomera "Isla Colombina." But there seems to be some

Garajonay covers ten percent of Gomera; in the distance looms Tenerife.

competition for this honor; others believe that Columbus uttered his final prayers before leaving the known world in a church on the isle of Gran Canaria.

Given Gomera's landmarks and historical niches, "Isla Colombina" could have been hyped to an extreme degree; instead, it is pleasantly low-key. After gazing at the six ornate altars in Gomera's lovely Asunción church, I wandered over to the adjoining Casa de Colón, the modestly traditional Gomeran house allegedly lent to Columbus during his stays on Gomera. The young curator of Casa de Colón seemed much more concerned with the erratic workings of his tape player than with delivering rote lectures on the significance of the monuments on Gomera and Columbus's three ships, displayed as finely crafted models in la casa. He did take the time, though, to whisper some risqué remarks about the famed explorer's carnal cavortings with Beatriz de Bobadilla, an attractive young widow and friend of the Spanish royal family. He said her peccadilloes back at court in Madrid had resulted in her banishment to Gomera, where she lived by the beach in a squat, square tower called Torre del Conde.

"Why else would Columbus keep coming to a place like Gomera—three times?" the curator asked me with a wink. Looking at the portrait of the beautiful Beatriz, which I had also noticed in my hotel, I tended to agree with him.

THOUGH NEGLIGIBLE in size as islands go, Gomera offers the explorer a remarkable range of diversions. Start with a drive due west past the soaring volcanic hill of 3,993-foot-high Roque de Agando, to Chipude. This small, bold town sits high on the southern edge of Garajonay National Park among ancient, terraced fields beneath the 4,100-foot basalt chimney of Fortaleza. From this flat summit, peering across the wild central mountainscape

of the island, the Guanche worshiped their nature gods at a central menhir said to date from 2500 B.C.

At El Cercado, the next village a mile or so down the road, island women use round basalt pebbles to shape and polish sun-dried bowls and pitchers on the steps of their homes, in the traditional Guanche manner and style.

Playa de Santiago on the south coast, with its picturesque fishing village and excellent beach, is Gomera's tourist center, but many prefer the less populous Valle de Gran Rey, ten miles to the south of El Cercado. This idyllic spot retains a subtropical spirit in its deep canyon, full of palm forests and terraced banana plantations ending in a gorgeous golden beach. I'd heard of the valley and its hippie-hangout reputation back in San Sebastián. Apparently it had now become a fashionable resort for young backpackers and affluent European "greens."

As I eased off the main island road into the Valle de Gran Rey, I expected the worst. Places can change so quickly: A freewheeling, monied generation, coupled with easy travel to almost anywhere, can make places like this valley vulnerable. Though the "improvements" of the last decade must surely have the original discoverers of this tiny nirvana churning in their hemp hammocks, the place is still amazingly mellow and pleasantly decadent. Yes, there were new houses, rental apartments, tiny budget hotels, and even a bungalow-villa complex; but such changes amounted to mere dabblings compared with the

Valle de Gran Rey

enormity of touristic outrages on the other Canary Islands.

It was hot here under the bright, direct sun. Very hot. I gulped down a beer at a small beachside café, then ran through the hot, dark sand, and flung myself—jeans and all—into the ocean surf. I whiled away the rest of the day trying not to notice the huddle of damsels in their monokinis with their watchful, bronzed companions. Maybe in a few years the place will be yet another "rack one up for the wreckers" resort, but so far not so bad.

Equally unmolested, Playa de Vallehermoso on the north coast nestles in a deep cleft below another enormous volcanic rise, and possesses a powerful beauty. Nearby, but fully visible only by boat, are the famous 300-foot-high columned basalt cliffs, Los Órganos, (the organ pipes). It's a long winding drive here from Roque de Agando, centerpoint of island roads, or from San Sebastián, but other villages merit a visit en route. These include Vallehermoso, clustered tightly below terraced fields and the basalt bulk of the 2,131-foot-high Roque Cano; Hermigua with its enormous volcanic monoliths that rise into the mist; and Santa Domingo, the site of a charming and historic monastery.

Agulo, one of the smallest villages of Gomera, and perhaps the most charming town on the entire island, boasts an idiosyncratic little church topped by six stubby Moorish domes. The village itself features narrow cobbled streets, tiny plazas, ornately balustraded balconies, and vast vistas of banana fields, ragged coastal cliffs, and tight, black coves.

Gomera truly rewards the unscheduled traveler, but a word of warning: Beware the temptations of the lush, primitive forest of Garajonay National Park, where visitors can easily become lost. This is no ordinary place. In fact, many of its flora and fauna are unique and are the last living specimens of species that lived more than 200 million years ago around the vast Sea of Tethys, the vestige of which is today's Mediterranean. Through a fortunate juxtaposition of high volcanic uplands, moisture-bearing trade winds, the constant presence of clouds, mists and rainfall, and natural reservoirs in the basalt bedrock, these species have continued to thrive. Indeed, the island has survived and flourished agriculturally through the building of terraces and the use of artesian wells to tap these vast reservoirs.

But back to the forest—in particular the 30-foot-high heather trees that cover the island's mountainous heart. A Yorkshireman familiar with the calf-high heather of the English and Scottish moors, I never suspected that the same species could grow to the height of trees—or that a Yorkshireman could disappear in that growth.

After all the serpentine driving I'd done to reach these mountainous heights, I decided to stretch my legs in the heather forest on a path marked by a rough wooden sign. Within seconds, the benign roadside landscape of feathery treetops became a chaos of contorted trunks and branches dripping with strings of straggly moss. A cold, clammy gloom enveloped me. The trees were so densely intertwined that sunshine penetrated only in thin shafts, falling on clumps of grotesque fungus and roots that writhed like angry pythons. It became dark; the path was hard to follow. I stumbled on basalt boulders and broken branches, moving ever deeper into darkness and unfamiliar landscape. I carefully judged each step so as not to lose the vague trail.

I remembered a warning sign by the roadside near Roque de Agando: "It is not advisable to leave the footway." As the path curled and swirled among the exposed roots, I began to doubt that I was still on the trail. Lacy, death-gray strands of moss brushed my face. A strange silence filled the murk. Then, out of nowhere, the mists edged in. Apparently that's the norm on Gomera—one minute bright sunshine, the next clinging mists that can smother the mountains for hours and sometimes days.

I'd had enough. I wanted to leave the forest to the real hikers who, back in San Sebastián, had regaled me with tales of week-long, lost-world expeditions into these strange mountains. I tried to re-trace my steps. Logic told me that if I started climbing, I'd eventually get back to the road, but everything looked new—not like the way I had come before. After an hour of unpleasant groping and blundering up slimy slopes through dense fog and suffocating humidity, I suddenly broke through a particularly thick tangle of heather trees to find the mountain road—flat, paved, and safe. A car passed. Someone laughed and waved. And as I removed the layers of clinging moss and the shards of bark from my head and clothes, I began laughing, too.

TRAVEL NOTES

CLIMATE: Balmy year-round, but wet in winter and occasionally scorching in July and August. Bring hiking boots and weather gear. **EASE OF ACCESS:** There are frequent ferries and car rentals in San Sebastián. Buses run often, but drive very slowly due to the vertical topography. **HIGHLIGHTS:** Garajonay National Park, a UNESCO World Heritage site, which has 400 rare plant species; Gomera's countless pristine beaches.

Indian Ocean

MAURITIUS

Poets and writers have found
heaven on this
French-flavored island.

ONE MIGHT expect a little purple prose from the French poet Charles Baudelaire, who described the island of Mauritius as "a perfumed country caressed by the sun." But then along came world-wandering author Mark Twain with his homage: "God made Mauritius first and then heaven. Heaven being copied from Mauritius."

How, I wondered, had such a tiny, oyster-shaped blip in the vast Indian Ocean—just 788 square miles, barely two-thirds the size of the state of Rhode Island—engendered such gushing from the normally taciturn Mr. Clemens?

Though skeptical that Mauritius could live up to such praise, I decided to go for a visit. Neither writer, I discovered, had exaggerated. The island was indeed beautiful, and I eagerly set out to explore it. Along the way islanders welcomed me into their lives—lives graced with languor, harmony, tranquility, and passion.

Mauritius lies in the Indian Ocean 1,200 miles off the eastern shores of Africa, 450 miles west of the island of Madagascar. Many of the European colonial powers controlled the island at one time or another: the Portuguese (loosely) in the early 1500s; the Dutch for more than a century from 1598; the French

for another century; and finally the British, from 1810 to 1968, when the island gained its independence.

Despite the ejection of the French in 1810, it is their spirit and cultural sophistication that still hold sway on Mauritius. The great sugar kings—the grands blancs who own 18 of the 19 vast plantations—are mainly Franco-Mauritian, and while other Europeans control much of the island's business, they are far less in evidence. Although Mauritius remains a member of the British Commonwealth and English is the official language, everyone speaks French (most also speak a colorful French-Bantu-Malagasy Creole) and seems to possess a Parisian-style grace and flair. The ethnic 17th- and 18th-century architecture that is left is decidedly French in its delicacy and trim. Towns with idiosyncratic French names are the norm—Curepipe, Deux Frères, Petit Paquet, Quartier Militaire, Quatre Soeurs. The basic tenets of French cuisine have been mixed with Indo-Mauritian, using curries and fiery tomato-based Creole sauces to create a fascinating blend of flavors.

The island's one million inhabitants—a fusion of Hindu, Tamil, Muslim, Chinese,

The surrounding coral reef can make ocean navigating difficult.

The isolated Le Morne Brabant once served as a refuge for slaves.

Creole, Franco-Mauritian, and European—are internationally known for living in racial and religious harmony (or, as suggested by one local cynic, "a harmonious separation"). Amid such cultural complexity are numerous religious denominations, about 87 of them, though Hinduism, Islam, and Christianity are the main faiths. Nearly everyone celebrates Christmas, and there is a mind-boggling array of other religious and ethnic festivals. The most spectacular of them, in a gory kind of way, is the Tamil Cavadee ceremony, which features penitents heavily skewered and/or hooked through cheeks, arms, ears, tongues, legs, and just about every other part of their bodies.

To OUTSIDERS, the island is best known for luxuriant beaches and resorts. My first night—in a resort at the northern tip of the island overlooking the perfect turquoise-blue oval of ocean at Grand Baie—made me realize why many of the tourists on the island spend most of their time enjoying the hedonistic ease of their hotels. The moon silvered the still sea as I pampered myself with a dip in the floodlit pool and then, on the terrace, had a cocktail the size of a birdbath and an exotically eclectic six-course dinner, followed by a display of erotic séga dances. Where once there had been decorous grace, good manners, and polite chitchat at the tables, the wild calypso rhythms and suggestive contortions of the sequined Mauritian beauties sent a tsunami of energy through the audience. Within seconds, passion had replaced proper behavior.

In the morning I was ready to go exploring, following whichever back roads seemed appealing. As I drove, a kaleidoscope of images

Young coconuts reward a successful climber.

flickered past: neatly uniformed schoolgirls around the bus stops; a gaudily-colored Tamil temple with writhing images of deities; Hindu houses marked by two flags on bamboo poles signifying purity and harmony; a Muslim temple, bright white with green trim, topped by two loudspeakers issuing the call to prayer; and next door a perfect replica of an English village church built of great slabs of lava basalt. Then there were the women: Indians in sparkling saris, Muslims in loose trousers, plump Creole matrons in bright Mauritian cloth dresses, and wizened Chinese grandmothers in silks selling candy and cookies to school kids from their bathroom-size *tabagie*, or corner stores.

Time-warp taxis—gleaming but ancient British-made Wolseleys and Austin Oxfords—were running up the long slope through the straggling town of Rose Belle onto the broad central plateau. Up here the air was cool, the wind fresh and full of ocean, the sky a sparkling blue. In every direction lay vast green swaths of sugarcane dotted with 40-foot-high mounds of basalt boulder. In the distance spiky, fanged mountains rose from sinuous morning mists floating above fields of bushy tea plantations.

I stopped at a small village market. Dozens of stalls shaded by canvas awnings were piled high with fresh-picked vegetables and fruit: papayas, mangoes, pineapples, oranges, bananas, coconuts, guavas, and scarlet bunches of freshly-picked litchis. An old Indian gentleman enticed me over to his enormous vat of boiling oil and offered me a crisp hot samosa. I ate one and then another. I left with a bag full of a mush of lentils wrapped in small pancakes (dal puri), a dozen tiny deep-fried balls of a spiced potato and chickpea mix (pakoras), and a pile of salty dried river shrimp (chevrettes)—the perfect match for a bottle of local Phoenix beer.

Finally I drove down the long slope and off the cool central plateau into the heat and clamor of the capital, Port Louis. In spite of its sophisticated offerings—restaurants with impressive gastronomic diversity; a small theater; the imposing Government House, built in 1822, set behind a stern gray statue of Queen Victoria; a scattering of modern commercial buildings; and a splendid park commemorating the 1988 visit of Pope Paul—Port Louis remains a pleasantly ramshackle place with Graham Greene overtones, crammed into a narrow valley between ragged mountains.

During the day, the prime focus of activity is the old market, where a redolent riot of flowers, fruit, vegetables, fish, meat, and spices can be found. After dusk I'd hoped for a venting of fresh life in this hot little town, but just the opposite happened. Once the offices and tabagies closed, by 6 p.m., the place seemed as dead as a dodo—an appropriate metaphor on Mauritius, for it was here, more than 300 years ago, that the Dutch destroyed this docile flightless bird along with the island's once abundant ebony forests.

A portion of Chinatown around Queen Street appeared to have the monopoly on nightlife. L'Amicale de Port Louis, a beloved Chinese gambling den sitting among lopsided tin-and-clapboard shacks and little Chinese restaurants with dim lights and a long list of daily specials, was a focal point. (A warning from personal experience: The odds are definitely not in your favor!)

THE NEXT morning I was at the Black River Gorge up on a rocky overview that offered a poignant reminder of how the island must have looked long before the Dutch came—before there were slaves or the French or the British, or any people at all. To reach this overview from Port Louis, I had driven the 25 miles south through Curepipe and crossed the scrub-jungle plateau of the Plaine Champagne, swerving to miss macaque monkeys. They had hopped out of the bushes to pick up some roadside morsel, then vanished again, faster than squirrels.

I left the car by the roadside and took a short walk through a stumpy forest to a cliff edge. Although the dodo is long gone, some of the world's rarest birds, such as the Mauritian pink pigeon and the Mauritian kestrel, can still be found on the island where they are now protected by a special wildlife fund. As I made my way to the cliff edge, I saw two rare, red-tailed paille-en-queue birds skim in gracious flight over the tops of traveler's palms and eucalyptus trees hundreds of feet below. A delicate waterfall tumbled off high ledges and filigreed down in rainbow sprays to disappear into the dense forest. In the distance lay the rocky cliffs of the southwest coast, more mountains, and beaches rimmed by an ocean glittering like hammered silver.

The place seemed to be the hidden heart of Mauritius. Something ancient, untouched, and wild.

Body piercings are part of a religious observance for a Tamil man.

And apparently it was. Later I spoke with a man clearing scrub from the edges of his small garden in a west coast village called Rivière Noire, located where the Black River emerges from its gorge and enters the ocean. "You wanna see somethin' real wild, man?" he asked me with a leer. "Real séga. Not that hotel stuff. The slave séga—fisherman séga. You c'mon down here Saturday nights, you really see somethin' special. Not for tourists. Just for us." I did, and it was.

The following day, a Monday, I went rambling among the surging hills of the eastern coast, south of the fabled resorts of Le Saint Géran and Le Touessrok. There were few beaches, but the serpentine road to Mahébourg was all mine as I wound around the tiny coves and the fishing villages below towering crags and spiring pinnacles. I paused by a small bay and sat in the shade of a banyan tree, watching the waves ease themselves over the beach pebbles. I sensed a slow gentling of my spirit.

A fisherman was crouched nearby, mending his nets. I joined him, watching his grandson hammer caulking into the sea-worn cracks of his small boat. The lovely languor of Mauritian Mondays, the unofficial Mauritan "extra-weekend," began to sink in. The fisherman told me about his life, a simple life in which 150 rupees a day ($15) was more than enough to buy a little meat, rice, a few eggplants, tiny cherry tomatoes, some cigarettes, and a bottle of island fruit wine.

"It is enough," he told me, "Why do I need more?"

For the rest of my time on the island, I blended indulgent hedonism—Mauritius begs you to pamper yourself—with serendipitous jaunts in my car to such places as the rocky terrain of the appropriately named region of Roche Terre, at the northern tip of the island. Here, among the now-familiar pyramid piles of rocks, the fields are divided into skinny strips of fertile ground separated by thick walls built of black boulders. Why had the locals gone to all that trouble for such meager slivers of land? Every year their arduous tilling turns up a fresh harvest of rocks. Yet they continue to clear and pile them; they continue to grow their corn and their sugarcane, living lives that appear to have changed little over the centuries.

Traditions, I finally realized, have sinews here, and the old ways endure because they are supported not by sentimentality but by long generations of quiet certainty.

"It is enough," I heard the fisherman's voice echo as I peered into an endless blue sky. And I understood exactly what he meant.

TRAVEL NOTES

CLIMATE: November to April has temperatures around 85°F; May to October, the Southern Hemisphere winter, is a little cooler. December to March can host tropical storms. Peak fishing season is between December and March, although it can extend late into May. **EASE OF ACCESS:** Direct flights from all over the globe. Or sail to the island, usually from southern Europe and Africa. Island roads are generally excellent; although rental cars and taxis can be expensive. **HIGHLIGHTS:** Snorkeling and scuba diving. Fishing for blue marlin, barracuda, and several species of sharks. The coastline is almost entirely surrounded by coral reefs.

Fiji

TAVEUNI

No sign of exotic tourist resorts here—
only mysterious places to explore
rather than tour.

I WENT to the Fiji Islands as an accidental tourist—actually, as a rather confused airline passenger. I was flying from Los Angeles to Sydney, Australia, and thought the stopover was to be Honolulu. It turned out to be Fiji—that legendary Pacific paradise of 300 tropical islands, 1,100 miles south of the Equator and 2,000 miles east of Sydney. I'd never given Fiji much thought, but as I peered out the window, I saw dozens of little palm-shrouded islets and atolls floating in a sapphire sea—a wondrous bouquet of wild places, each island edged by pink and gold sand. Most seemed uninhabited—tiny tropical paradises. And in the hazy distance, I saw more of them fading into a blue-on-blue horizon. I decided to stay awhile.

We landed at Nadi, the gateway town for the Fiji Islands, on the main island of Viti Levu. After a night in this rowdy international hub of the South Pacific, I needed to find a quieter island in the archipelago. Perhaps an island with mountains, inexpensive hotels, waterfalls, lovely beaches, and interesting people—a place small enough to explore in a few days.

Which is how I came to Taveuni.

Third largest of the Fijian archipelago, the "garden isle" is about 28 miles long and an average of six miles wide, with a population of around 12,000 people, consisting mainly of Fijians and a substantial number of Indians, who appear to run most of the island businesses.

Dramatically profiled, Taveuni has a dragon-back spine of 3,000-foot-high volcanic cones cloaked in thick green forests. Below are tiny bays arced with bright white sand; flashes of waterfalls tumbling from the ridges; scatterings of cottages with palm-frond roofs; and large coconut-palm plantations. Above are sinewy paths that trail into dense forests, where the air is thick and intensely scented, and you can see tatters of clouds trailing off Mount Uluiqalau, the island's highest peak at more than 4,040 feet. Then there are the ragged, surf-fringed reefs, which offer some of the finest scuba diving in the South Pacific. No sign of exotic tourist resorts here—only mysterious places to explore.

Looking into the shining, smiling eyes of a typical Fijian today, it's hard to imagine the great wars that were once fought between and across these islands. Tales of ritual slaughters, sacrifices, and feasting on the bodies of enemies abound. Then there were the guile, cunning, and open graft of intertribal conflicts; the grudges that set clan against clan for centuries; and the

Schoolchildren saunter through a plantation.

Showering falls echo in a quiet forest on Taveuni.

unfortunate fates of so many island women, strangled by their own sons so that they might accompany their husbands into the afterlife.

Intrusion of the West and western values came slowly in the wake of such notable explorers as Abel Tasman (1643), James Cook (1774), and the unfortunate Captain William Bligh, who was pursued through the archipelago in 1789 by armed tribesmen in huge *druas* (canoes). Bligh and his 18 loyal officers of the H.M.S. *Bounty* were set adrift by mutineers off Fiji's coast. They would have met death among the treacherous reefs had it not been for sudden storms and other fortuitous occurrences that enabled them to escape the bloodthirsty Fijians. After more than 40 days on the open ocean, they reached the Dutch island of Timor, more than 4,000 miles west of Fiji. Despite all the horrors of this amazing journey, Bligh made charts of the Bligh Islands, as he called Fiji, which were used for almost a century by other explorers and traders.

At first, the Fijians regarded such intruders with suspicion and resentment, but as the wealth from these outsiders increased, the Fijians willingly allowed them to gather precious sandalwood and later the odd but oh-so-valuable bêche-de-mer (sea cucumber) in exchange for muskets and mercenary assistance during the almost constant tribal conflicts. Even the early English missionaries turned out to be useful military advisors, helping the Fijian Chief Cakabau decimate the fierce Tongan invaders in the mid-1800s and liberate the Fiji Islands. After that, the chiefs began to give up their cannibalistic ways, becoming ardent Christians under relatively benevolent British colonialism. The drinking of kava—a favorite national brew made domestically from either the powdered or mouth-masticated yaqona plant—replaced the customs of ferocious cults.

MY FIRST days on Taveuni were blue and cloudless. The water in the bays sparkled, the palms by the roadside wafted in warm breezes, and the sun poured drunkenly over everything. There were fishermen offshore in dugout canoes carved from single tree trunks. Night-black myna birds squawked in the bushes. Children played in the surfy shallows and waved when

Snorkelers adventure along a coral reef near Taveuni.

they saw my pink, sun-scorched face. I waved back and heard their calls of "*vinaka, vinaka—*thank you, thank you"—echo through the trees.

I took up residence in the Garden Island Resort at Waiyevo, an attractive and modestly priced hotel about halfway down the western coast, 12 miles or so from the airstrip. Here the days slipped by gently. From time to time there were sudden storms, thick black curtains of rain sweeping across a sky punctuated by brilliant shafts of sunlight that made the roadside hibiscus and frangipani shimmer.

On a nearby beach I discovered a sign proclaiming that I now stood astride the international dateline—the 180th meridian—so I bounced from Tuesday into Wednesday and back into Tuesday and smiled at what a funny thing time is. Only later did I learn that the sign was a little outdated and that the official dateline had been redrawn to curve around Fiji, keeping all the islands on the same time.

On Taveuni, however, timekeeping seemed irrelevant. I discarded my watch and marked the days' progress by the movement of the sun over the high volcanic ridges. If it became too hot, I wandered off into the forest dappled with musty light. Parrots, honeyeaters, and fan-tailed cuckoos floated in and out of the trees. (Taveuni is one of the best bird-watching locations in Fiji.) If it rained that silky, warm island rain while I was hiking, I'd lie on the ground and let it soak me with its freshness.

One day I passed a village market, a casual sprawl of rickety tables and blankets spread on the ground. In addition to the rainbow-hued mounds of just-caught fish, I saw baskets brimming with shiny papaws, mangoes, clusters of burgundy-red grapes, and great orange moons of halved pumpkins scooped out and ready to eat. On separate tables were the muscular, bulbous shapes of yams, breadfruit, taro, cassava, and rich purple dalo. And of course the inevitable yaqona wrapped in torn sheets of the Fiji Times and awaiting the ritual pounding for innumerable kava celebrations.

A FEW days later I hitchhiked to the imposing Wairiki Mission church. There I got a ride with some fishermen heading for the southern tip of the island to visit friends in Navakawau (end of the road) village. They invited me to join them. We drove on the edge of rugged cliffs and past an enormous blowhole, then we crossed plateaus of exposed lava flows in which there are deep tunnels where the Taveunians once buried their fiercest warriors. "When they died it was a secret," one of the fishermen, Tabu (a shortened version of Tabucakua), told me. "They didn't want their enemies to know, so they hid them in these tunnels."

After a couple of bone-jarring hours, we arrived in Navakawau. The village was filled with a colorful collection of brightly painted cottages and traditional bures scattered around a central dusty space. I expected the men to go off fishing with their friends, but they had other, far more important things in mind—kava-drinking and impromptu meke sessions of clapping songs and storytelling.

In the good old kava-drinking ceremonies, the roots of yaqona pepper plants were chewed into a soft, pulpy mix by village virgins and spat into a huge bowl to which water was added. Today's ritual lacks much of the original mystique and charm—maybe it's the diminished supply of virgins or merely the convenience of packaged yaqona powder.

But I quickly learned that the tradition included lots of clapping, shouting, and smiling. The kava itself was nothing overwhelming or mind-blowing—or so I thought. Just a tingle on the lips and on the tongue, a slight relaxing of muscles, a smile that increased with each cup. The taste? Well, it was a mix of cold, mint-flavored tea and diluted mud. I was increasingly amused as I tried, unsuccessfully, to stroll around the village or to speak. I felt buoyed by a spirit of utter happiness and I felt welcome everywhere I went.

In the days after my return from the kava bout, I wandered randomly around the small island. I came to Bouma Falls, a series of three cascades hidden deep in the northern part of the rain forest. I sketched the first 60-foot-high cascade and then stripped and dived into the pool at the base of the falls. I floated on my back and listened to the roar of the water. Taveuni, as you might surmise, was one more secret place I found hard to leave.

TRAVEL NOTES

CLIMATE: It's usually hot, and humid. November to May is the wet season.
EASE OF ACCESS: Buses along the northern coast have erratic schedules; rental cars are for the adventurous. Hitchhiking is customary. **HIGHLIGHTS:** Secluded white sand beaches; climbing to Lake Tagimaucia; boating to outer islands.

Australia

HINCHINBROOK

Despite the efforts of settlers,
the island remains intact, inviolate,
and very inviting.

WRITERS HAVE described Australia's Great Barrier Reef island of Hinchinbrook as "a chunk of pure, unadulterated New Guinea that somehow floated south across Torres Strait." Other writers have celebrated this spot as "the most beautiful place on Earth" and "true Robinson Crusoe territory." All, it seems, agree that the island is a breathtaking tapestry of mountains, rain forests, vast mangrove swamps, untouched tracts of pine and hardwoods, unsullied gold- and white-sand beaches, cool streams and pools, lacy waterfalls, and some of the most pristine landscapes to be found—anywhere.

The Great Barrier Reef, off the northeastern coast of Australia, is a 1,240-mile-long stretch of coral reefs, sandbar cays, and islands. It is revered not only as the world's largest oceanic national park, but the largest structure on the planet built by living organisms. It is one of the few places on Earth to receive double World Heritage status. This magnificent ecosystem is home to more than 2,000 species of fish and countless species of mollusks, sponges, crustaceans, and echinoderms—all living and breeding among 500 different kinds of hard and soft coral. Every year new species of fish are found.

English explorer James Cook recorded the location of the island on June 8, 1770, but erroneously (and uncharacteristically) considered it part of the mainland. He failed to spot the narrow, 30-mile-long mangrove-edged channel at the southern end that separates Hinchinbrook from the coast. A later sailor found the sandbanks and shoals around the island so treacherous that he wrote, "No one can sail through the Hinchinbrook Pass and not believe in God."

Hinchinbrook, at a size of approximately 250 square miles, has a status as the largest island national park in the world. It is home to 6 types of frog, 4 of turtle, 17 of lizard, 11 of snake, and 149 kinds of bird—but, fortunately, only one species of saltwater crocodile. The number of saltwater crocodiles in most places is so low that those in the park could be considered a potential source of stock for the species.

Hinchinbrook's importance as an ecologically pristine national park means that serious hikers must make a special effort to explore here. Park authorities carefully regulate permits, campsites, and seasonal use. Along the 22-mile, three- to four-day East Coast Hike from George Point at the southern tip of the island to Ramsay Beach (and, optionally, from there to

Roots of mangroves on Hinchinbrook's beaches help prevent erosion.

Cape Richards), facilities are virtually nonexistent; the only thing available is an abundance of nature's own clear, fresh water. It is also a tough slog if you throw in a climb up the island's dominant and dramatically profiled monolith, 3,700-foot-high Mt. Bowen.

Less active vacationers looking for something a little different will enjoy the refurbished Hinchinbrook Island Resort at the northern tip of the wild Cape Richards promontory. The resort offers the only formal accommodations on the island. But even here phones, faxes, TVs, and all the hoopla of hotels worldwide are sacrificed for peace, silence, tranquility, and a chance to get in touch with a little corner of wild Earth.

It is remarkable that such a sophisticated resort managed to survive on the island at all. Hinchinbrook has a reputation for eluding the plans and schemes of modern man. Early on, the resort—a tiny enclave of 16 acres—saw hurricanes and wrecked seaplanes. The Aboriginals—1,000 or so Bandyin people—existed here happily for thousands of years, but as soon as the Europeans started nosing around in the 19th century, the island itself seemed to demonstrate a determination to resist outsiders.

As settlers crept up the Queensland coast, a few thought Hinchinbrook a fine place for colonization. So they came. They tried a little cattle ranching, citrus growing, lumbering, and lime crushing using the ancient Aboriginal shell middens, but one by one they were beaten back and bankrupted—their spirits bowed by the intransigence of the place. One ambitious missionary settled here and stayed for a year, but the Aboriginals shunned him and he went mad, unbalanced by the solitude and silence.

BUT THAT kind of "unbalance" worked fine for me. What happens when you give yourself the gift of pure, uncluttered time? What happens, of course, is pure magic. Days when all you have to do is wander rain-forest trails, watch animals at play, sense the slow passage of the day through an arcing sun and a moon sliding across velvet-black skies full of unfamiliar star patterns. Preconceptions fade, and the unfiltered beauty of a place takes over.

Hinchinbrook

Brian Edmunds, the cheerful manager of the island resort that I visited, summed up the "Hinchinbrook Hook": "It gets inside you...deep inside. Something changes. You become a different person—maybe even a better person, if you're lucky!"

My first day at the resort was delightfully decadent. I enjoyed my tree-house chalet, reached by a long wooden staircase through the branches and leaves, and the bounty of the open-air dining room. I took a swim in the pool, a leisurely stroll along the beach, and a couple of wandering walks in the shadowy rain forest immediately outside my door.

On the second day, I was ready to begin my explorations. In a small boat, I headed for the humid, shadowy channels of the mangrove swamps of Missionary Bay on the westward side of Hinchinbrook's forked northern extremity.

It is said that more than 30 kinds of mangrove trees grow here, but my neophyte eyes were aware only of the hypnotic homogeneity of the swamp itself. Gurgling and plopping sounds—the spasmodic burbling of a crocodile, or some other predator I had not learned about?—turned out to be gas bubbles of decaying vegetation, which provides rich nutrients for the fish living and spawning in the bay. And those loud, firecracker retorts from the darkness? As I later learned, they were the snapping claws of burrowing mud prawns.

Shafts of hazy sunlight filtered through the dense canopy of mangrove leaves, whose texture ranged from emery paper to the finest of sheened satins. Fiddler crabs scuttled among the labyrinths of vegetation, and I saw two mudskippers—strange goggle-eyed fish that climb among the exposed mangrove roots and can even cover considerable distances on land with their limb-like fins. A great blue heron stood as still and erect as a worn wooden post, awaiting a passing lunchtime fish. Kingfishers, yellow-breasted sunbirds, and whimbrels skittered and flitted among the branches.

Much later, as I was easing down the channel back toward Missionary Bay, my jaunt ended in a little magic and mystery. Ahead of my boat, maybe 50 yards or so, part of a huge gray-brown creature with a smooth, water-sheened skin emerged slowly from the still water, rolled a little, emitted a soft sighing sound, and then quietly submerged again.

I wondered at first whether it was a bottlenose dolphin, a species that frequents these parts, but then I realized I hadn't seen a dorsal fin. Or maybe it was a tiny portion of a humpback whale. I'd heard that this nutrient-rich bay was one of their favorite nurturing places on their long annual journeys to the Antarctic breeding grounds. But no—it was too small and the wrong color. So I concluded with delight that I had been presented with a brief sighting of the endangered dugong—that rare, 9-foot-long, 700-pound mammal whose strange, female-like features are said to be the origins of many ancient mermaid myths. These dugongs are endangered because of their inclination to swim in shallow, inshore waters, which brings them in contact with humans. Even the smallest dugong population change affects their survival since they have such a low reproduction rate. Back at the resort, Edmunds told me that "there used to be huge herds of them all over Rockingham Bay. Now it's a real treat if you manage to see one."

THE NEXT day I took a short walk through the rain forest to North Shepherd Beach. I could have continued on a longer half-day trail to South Shepherd Beach, but distance was not the point of the walk. What I really wanted was a period of languid peace to experience the richness and variety of the island's northern rain forest. And what variety I found! In the humid stillness of filtered sunlight I spotted, among the Rousseau-like tumult of vegetation, huge buttress-rooted quandong trees, gums, oaks, mahoganies, turpentines, satin ashes, bloodwoods, paperbarks, strangler figs, and ironbarks

all rising out of a dense understory of pandanus, grasstree cycads, and sprinklings of cabbage and fan palms that added colorful and delicate contrast.

On my last day I joined a group from the resort and went snorkeling off the Brook Islands, a small cluster of low-lying coral islets five miles or so northeast of Cape Richards. The ocean teemed with surf parrot fish, butterfly, neonfish, and scores of other brilliantly colored species that swooped among the multishaped bomb, brain, sea fan, staghorn, and other exotic corals. There I spotted the sensually inviting, diaphanous blue-and-gold-flecked "lips" of huge giant clams, some more than four feet across.

Drifting with my snorkel over the satiny, sun-dappled shallows, I could feel the warmth of the sun on my back and the wavelets lapping my outstretched arms. I felt utterly weightless. Buoyed by a benevolent ocean, lost in random reverie, I felt that I could float like this forever.

TRAVEL NOTES

CLIMATE: Avoid the heat and humidity and travel during the June-to-August winter when average daily temperatures are temperate. **EASE OF ACCESS:** Access to the island is limited to regular ferry and other boats out of Cardwell on the mainland. The Hinchinbrook Island Resort is 15 miles east of Cardwell on Cape Richards. **HIGHLIGHTS:** Silence and solitude in a virtually untouched tropical island national park and World Heritage site. A chance to snorkel among the giant clams or spot an elusive dugong.

Japan

GENKAI

In the end, serendipity
leads to an enchanting place
that redefines gastronomy.

HUNTING FOR secret places can be a fickle business. I invariably burden myself with arduous research, talk to countless world wanderers, gushy advisers at tourist offices, and informed locals. Finally I make my choice, and off I go, hoping the selected place lives up to my enthusiastic expectations.

In the end, serendipity wins out over plans and schedules. You cast yourself upon uncharted tides in a misty sea, exactly as I did on Japan's southernmost island, Kyūshū, lovingly known as the Old Japan.

My original plans were quite clear. The intended secret-place destination was to be somewhere along a looping route on the Korea Strait east from Fukuoka, Kyūshū's largest and most vibrantly modern city situated around the broad arc of Hakata Bay in the northwest corner of the island. My plan was to wander through the tangled riot of jungled mountains in the heart of the island to the world's largest caldera, Mount Aso. According to my notes, this region had it all—splendidly dramatic scenery, traditional ryokans (small inns), natural hot spring onsen baths, ancient legends of the Sun God (Japan's founding deity), the great, shadowy gorges of Takachiho, and active volcanoes

spuming steam and occasional fiery lava burps. What more could one ask?

But then along came a very friendly Mr. Yamamoto as I strolled the oceanfront park at Fukuoka, and everything changed. We chatted awhile about the delights and diversions of this city of 1.3 million. We discussed its new and imaginatively designed shopping complexes, excellent museums, ancient temples, the beautiful gardens of Ohori Park, the bizarre nightlife in the entertainment district of Nakasu, and—of course—the scores of unique little yatai, food stalls that emerge out of nowhere every evening along downtown streets and attract hundreds of loyal local devotees until the early hours of the morning.

"Oh, yes," he replied to my enthusiastic listing of the city's main attractions, "Very, very nice. But, please, excuse me for asking...of course you may have other plans...and I do not want to delay your departure in any way..." He swallowed hard and went for broke. "Genkai!" He said the word with obvious great relief. "I wonder if you have some time to visit our little hidden island of Genkai. It's not very far by boat from our harbor here, maybe half an hour on the new ferry."

A small bridge leads to a part of paradise on Kyūshū Island.

A Genkai fishmonger displays the catch of the day.

And that's when serendipity took over. I abandoned my plan and a couple of hours later I boarded a small and virtually empty ferry at Bayside Place on Fukuoka's harbor. We headed west across Hakata Bay, in the direction of South Korea, through damp mists on unpleasantly rolling waters.

"Genkai not far, but maybe not see," suggested a friendly ferry attendant. He was right. Then, out of a gossamer mist floating above the ocean rose a perfect cone—a miniature Mount Fuji, bathed in spring sunshine, green and lush.

"Ah—the home of Yuri Waka."

"Excuse me?" I said, turning to see a beaming-faced gentleman at my side, gazing along with me at the emerging island.

"It is place of an ancient legend. This little island is quite important historically. Many stories here," he continued.

To meet two English-speaking Japanese in one morning was a rare event. The man turned out to be a professor emeritus at Kyūshū University and an avid admirer of the 700-foot-high island cone ahead of us. He often came to Genkai, he told me, to fish and stroll around the two-mile circular basalt-and-granite island. He admired its untouched wild nature, resplendent with rape blossoms in spring, silk trees in summer, wild chrysanthemums in autumn, and vast swaths of golden daffodils in late winter.

"Only 800 people or so living there now," he told me. "Mostly fishermen families. The seas around those smaller basalt column islands"—he pointed to a scattering of cave-pocked rocky extrusions now also appearing out of the mist—"are very rich in marine life. They can collect many abalone, sea urchins, turbot, shrimp—make good living here."

Then, as I had hoped, he told me the wonderful island tale of Yuri Waka, son of a high court official during the reign of the Saga Emperor (A.D. 809–823). In typical Japanese fashion, the tale is full of symbolism and layered in meaning. But in movie-script distillation, it describes the courageous Yuri Waka's successful three-year conquest and annihilation of the murderous, plundering pirates who dominated the Korea Strait and the southwestern coast of the Korean peninsula.

Returning home as a hero, Yuri graciously allowed his fighting ship crews to rest awhile on Genkai before sailing on to accept his reward and accolades at the emperor's castle on the mainland. But two of his adjutant generals, the Befu brothers, thought that they deserved these honors instead. So, while praising Yuri's great feats, they doused him with sake (rice wine), and as he was sleeping off his stupor, they marooned him on Genkai and returned to the mainland, mourning Yuri's death in a last ferocious battle with the pirates. Thus they received Yuri's honors and even tried to seduce his wife in endless bouts of debauchery and drunkenness at court.

The loyal Princess Kasuga did not believe the brothers' story. In a convoluted series of attempts to find Yuri (the story involves Yuri's pet messenger hawk and other intriguing intricacies), she managed to ensure his return with him disguised as a peasant. The grand climax came at a New Year's archery contest when Yuri, still in disguise, bellowed with laughter at the Befu brothers' amateurish performances. Handed a bow as a challenge, Yuri immediately killed both brothers with a single arrow, reclaimed his loyal princess, and belatedly accepted his honors.

"There is a special shrine—Kotaka—on the island," the professor told me. "It is very beautiful. You go under the large torii gate and up a long series of steps (typical of Shinto shrines). It is to honor Yuri's messenger hawk, Midori-maru, sent by the princess to find him. You should go there."

So THAT, of course, became my first island destination. As we nudged the dock I thanked my professor-informant. He left for his day of fishing and I set off into the little village clustered in dense layers up the steep slope of the island. Actually it was very, very steep. Nothing but steps climbing up narrow alleyways between traditional fishermen's homes adorned with flowering plants, and with elaborate miniature red-and-gold Buddhist "good fortune" shrines set near their front doors. It was utterly breathtaking (in the aesthetic as well as physical sense). Never had I seen such a place in Japan. It reminded me of an Italian hill village with its serpentine lanes, tightly packed homes, colorful lines of drying clothes waving in sea breezes, the delicious aromas of food cooking in tiny kitchens, and the chatter of voices behind high walls and hedges.

I was entranced by the place. I peered through the hedges, across compact gardens immaculately landscaped with small bushes, bonsai, carefully pruned trees, moss-sheened rocks, and small reflecting pools. I could see traditional tatami-floored rooms sparsely furnished with low tables, cushions, wall scrolls, and delicate shoji—unique sliding rice-paper panels used as exterior walls and as interior room dividers. They are immensely practical, providing ventilation and the flexible use of a house's total living space—giving a small house many different looks and enabling the creation of instant futon bedrooms or large family dining areas whenever required.

I kept on climbing, sometimes pausing to sketch, then climbing again. Women passed with enormous wicker baskets on their bonnet-shrouded heads, or even larger wooden contraptions on their backs that were locally known as oi. Both were used for carrying nets, food supplies, propane bottles, and just about everything else (there are few delivery vans in this almost vertical

Paper carp streamers

community). Children dressed in their neat regulation school uniforms, with little red leather backpacks, scampered down the alleys from the school set high on a bluff.

One precocious young boy paused to watch me sketch and very carefully enunciated: "Hello. I think that is very nice. Goodbye." Then he leaped down the steps after his friends, excitedly bragging that he'd spoken English to a gai-jin (foreigner) and escaped unscathed. (Gai-jin are still treated a little cautiously in Japan.)

Unsure of the Kotaka shrine's precise location, I stopped at one of the island's two traditional ryokans to ask directions. The family was in the midst of preparing lunch and asked if I'd like to join them. When I accepted (hewing to my creed of never rejecting spontaneous opportunities), they expressed their delight in unexpected tsunamis of enthusiasm.

Pointing to a large fish-filled glass tank outside the front door, the lady of the house—an imposing matron with a broad toothy smile—asked me which of the colorful swimming creatures I'd like to eat. My appetite abruptly diminished, but I'd already accepted their invitation so I reluctantly pointed to one particularly succulent-looking fish. She promptly scooped it up with a sieve along with something else that resembled a gelatinous sausage, rather sticky and squirmy. I squirmed too, anthropologically speaking, but I was curious to see what she planned to do with her captive fish.

If not exactly memorable, lunch was certainly different from my normal ramen-noodle and stir-fry vegetable repasts. First came scalding seafood soup, full of fish bits and pieces floating in a pungent broth made golden by sea urchin roe. It tasted of pure ocean. Then cold slices of a slimy thing arrived, which turned out to be a sea cucumber, considered a delicacy in these parts. It was virtually tasteless and unpleasantly jellylike, but a little soy sauce and hot green wasabi helped get it down, as they did with the freshest of fresh ikeuo-style sashimi (thinly cut raw slices of live fish) from my selected tank occupant.

A large bowl of hot sticky rice, two enormous poached prawns, and tiny cups of green tea brought me back into more familiar territory. A big squishy bun filled with sweet bean paste arrived as dessert on an enormous plate along with a welcome flask of warm sake.

My hostess asked if I was staying overnight on the island. I hadn't decided at that point, but when she proudly gave me a tour of her little ryokan and showed me a beautiful tatami room with a balcony overlooking the village and the harbor filled with fishing boats, I knew I'd be staying. Right there.

There was no rush now. No mad dash for the last ferry of the day. There was just me, this intriguing island, my tranquil ryokan room—and, once again, abundant time.

I eventually found the Kotaka shrine to Yuri Waka's beloved hawk, Midori-maru. It was set in typical Shinto fashion atop a long flight of steps above the torii gate, as the professor had described, and consisted of *haiden* and *honden*, the typical dual building-style shrine. Each building was delicately carved in unpolished, unpainted wood and set in a shady grove of trees with inscribed boulders and coiled *shimenawa* ropes surrounding sacred features of the site. White paper streamers (*gohe*) were placed everywhere to lure the wandering spirit of the shrine (*kami*) back to its home in the honden.

I paused awhile to enjoy the peace and silence of Kotaka, then began my island explorations, which continued for the next couple of days. Beyond an adjoining and colorful, ornate Buddhist temple, a narrow path laced with large flat stones wound up alongside tiny plots of sweet potatoes, taro, and onions, ultimately leading me to Genkai's summit. The views were spectacular here, particularly of the bold little basalt-columned offshore islets and—in the hazy distance—the faint outline of Fukuoka's dramatic, ultramodern skyline. Strange mounds and distinct rocks at the summit are said to mark ancient tombs. An unexpected pocket of woodland offered welcome shade and silence.

Another path I took later in the day wriggled its way around the base of the island, passing two small sandy beaches and great boulders of white granite and black basalt on which cormorants and sea hawks perched. With the exception of the occasional lone recreational fisherman, I had the place to myself and constantly enjoyed the delightful contrast between the wild paths with their ancient inscribed stones, the secluded bays, and the compact, colorful intensity of the village itself. There I discovered a second shrine, Wakamiya, between the elementary and junior high schools, where villagers came to pray for the safety of their fishermen. Another quiet and moving place.

Islands can be sneaky places—places where you feel intensely elsewhere. They wiggle their way into your spirit with offerings of sweet latency and a calming, nurturing atmosphere, not often found in mainland places. They seduce you into the appreciation of unfamiliar delights. I mean—can you believe it?—on the second day I was even developing a taste for sliced raw sea cucumber...without the soy and wasabi.

TRAVEL NOTES

CLIMATE: Avoid the winter, when it can be chilly and wet; the humid heart of high summer (August); and the rainy season of June and July. **EASE OF ACCESS:** A 30 minute ferry ride from Kyūshū's largest city of Fukuoka. **HIGHLIGHTS:** Seclusion, shrines, serendipity, and Ikeuo cuisine, including sea cucumbers.

Mountains and

A sea of salt deposits rises from the Atacama Desert.

Deserts

United States

HELLS CANYON

This is the kind of place
that makes all my wanderings
feel worthwhile.

"IT'S A kid's dream come true," said six-foot-tall, bearded David Manuel—artist, sculptor, historian, collector, and raconteur. "I'm the kid—and here's my dream!" Smiling, he held out his arms to encompass the massive log-beam interior of his Nez Perce Crossing Museum, art gallery, and sculpture showroom in Joseph—a town of 1,250 inhabitants nestled more than 4,000 feet high at the base of Oregon's towering Wallowa Mountains. Already it was early summer, but a few tips of the 10,000-foot peaks of the 360,000-acre Eagle Cap Wilderness were still white with snow. At the edge of town, a broad, green valley eased out into close-cropped horse pastures, wheat fields, and grasslands dotted with barns and grazing cows.

"The Nez Perce were always my favorite people, ever since I found their arrowheads as a boy along the Columbia River," recalled David. "This was all part of their territory. They called it The Valley of the Winding Waters. They were wiped out in 1877 when they were driven 1,400 miles north to the Canadian border along what is now called the Nez Perce National Historic Trail. And all because they refused to leave their own treaty lands. A real tragedy—which ended in those famous words of Young Joseph,

leader of the tribe: 'My heart is sick and sad…. I will fight no more forever.'"

One of David's most impressive sculptures was an enormous bronze statue of Young Chief Joseph, standing proudly outside the museum, gazing across the vistas that were once part of his homeland. Inside the gallery were more bronze sculptures and paintings of Indians and other Remington-style Western subjects. There were also dozens of museum cases filled with David's amazing collections of Indian tribal artifacts.

"Well, all this is mainly thanks to my wife, Lee," David explained. "She keeps me and the Valley Bronze going. Can you believe how all this has happened in an out-of-the-way little place like Joseph? Twenty years back it was all tumbleweed and tumbledown. Now we've got half a dozen foundries here and so many artists, sculptors, and writers—even a big annual writer's conference with the nonprofit organization Fishtrap , and festivals galore. It seems a bit like New York at times!" He laughed. "Well, until you step outside and see where we are."

AND WHERE we were was picture-perfect. The mountains were calling, so I took a

Hells Canyon reigns as the deepest canyon in the United States.

United States

GREEN MOUNTAINS

Robert Frost's poetry and spirit
permeate the region's deep forests
and old mountains.

THE VIBRANTLY colored hand-painted sign read: "Make Love Not War." It had been a couple of decades since I'd seen that memorable motto of the flower-power era. Yet it still seemed appropriate for Bristol, with its spirit of easygoing community cohesiveness, its creativity, and its Victorian appearance. The latter takes the form of a redbrick 19th-century main street, a spacious town green with an ornate bandstand, and some fine Gothic homes sprinkled along side streets.

The small town of Bristol, the starting point of my journey through Vermont's Green Mountains, lies high in the northern foothills, 30 miles south of Burlington and about 200 miles northwest of Boston. Soaring high above the town is the Bristol Cliffs Wilderness Area, a special part of the Green Mountain National Forest, maintained as a primitive roadless tract.

On this trip I took the open road through one of the most beautiful parts of New England in the company of a revered man of letters. I was bumping along forest-shaded back roads in a region locally known as Frostland. And it was indeed the spirit and sentiments of poet Robert Frost, winner of four Pulitzer Prizes, that imbued my journey with a deeper resonance.

Even for those who are relative strangers to the words of that crusty New England poet-farmer, lines from one of his best-known works, "The Road Not Taken," echo in the recesses of the heart:

> Two roads diverged in a wood, and I—
> I took the one less traveled by,
> And that has made all the difference.

Such sentiments surely appeal to those hobo-selves lingering in the wings of our lives, waiting for a chance to roam, to take chances, and to celebrate Frost's affirmations that spirit-guided choices at critical junctures of our lives can make "all the difference."

Certainly in this spectacular part of the Green Mountains, renowned particularly for its brilliant fall foliage and, way to the northeast, for the excellence of its skiing, choices abound in terms of wanderings. Though I began my explorations in Bristol, others may choose to start their journeys 12 miles farther south at Middlebury, nexus of eight highways. Here, you'll find a spacious green with bandstand, prominent churches and inns, a gracious Old World main street, the spectacular Otter Creek

A waterfall tumbles in Vermont's Green Mountain National Forest.

waterfall right in the center of town, and even a town brewery of the same name. There's also the prime attraction of Middlebury College. Founded in 1800 as a liberal arts college, it subsequently became a catalyst for the establishment of notable museums, art galleries, theaters, a craft center, a folk-life center, and the nearby University of Vermont's Morgan Horse Farm.

One of Middlebury's most noted worldwide contributions is the Bread Loaf School of English. The private school boasts three international locations in addition to the original site up in the mountains east of Middlebury, near the hamlet of Ripton, on what is known as The Robert Frost Memorial Drive. I took a drive up to the school, which is the heart, the true focus, of Frostland. Not only did the poet cofound this venerable institution in 1920 and found the Bread Loaf Writers' Conference in 1926, but he also spent many of his summers hidden away nearby in a forest cabin on the Homer Noble farm in Ripton, where he wrote several volumes of his works.

Nearby is one of my favorite spots—the Robert Frost Trail. Here, boardwalk and earth paths meander for a half mile or so through scrub brush and marshes. Here you can enjoy the untrammeled displays of raw nature and a

Autumn in Vermont

selection of Frost's poems on plaques placed every 50 yards or so along the trail. I scribbled one strange but beguiling excerpt in my notebook: "We dance around in a ring and suppose. But the secret sits in the middle and knows."

IMMEDIATELY TO the south of Bread Loaf lies the 20,000-acre Moosalamoo—a continuation of the Bread Loaf Wilderness to the north and a wonder-world of rugged cliffs and mountains, hidden lakes and streams. It was home to the Missisquoi band of the Abenaki Indians before the disruptive incursions of European settlers in the early 1700s. According to a brochure I picked up, Frost's summers in these parts were spent "finding inspiration and solitude." Among these silent forests and crags—the haunt of black bears, moose, and peregrine falcons—and along the winding trails, he observed the secretive behaviors of the animals as they foraged for food, rested in the sun, and looked for mates. Once, while watching the "uncaged progress of a bear," Frost penned the following stern reminder to our supposedly superior species:

The world has room to make a bear feel free;
The universe seems cramped to you and me.

FROSTLAND IS a seductive region. You begin to sense the theme that threads through so much of his poetry—that our insignificance seems to be directly proportionate to the significance we bestow upon ourselves.

I decided it was time to go exploring deeper into the mountains. Ripton's lopsided general store was a great place to start. A snaking gravel road leads north for ten miles or so to Lincoln through wild, lake-laced forests and hollows. Benefiting from Frost's constant reproaches to us mortals about pacing and racing and never resting, I drove as slowly as I pleased. About halfway along the track, I heard the sound of roaring water. I parked the car and got out. As I strolled through the woods toward the source of the sound—it turned out to be a beautiful waterfall—the peace of the place flowed in like lazy waves, washing away all the crud and clutter, the accumulated mental junk of months.

The next part of my drive was up the unpaved track of the 2,424-foot-high Lincoln Gap. Local lore tells of unfortunates trapped on these wind-scoured heights during unpredictable snowstorms—some as late as May. My journey was not traumatic, merely one of the most exhilarating driving experiences in Vermont.

Warren, at the eastern end of the Lincoln Gap road, is not altogether unaware of its traditional white-clapboard charms. Yet despite the array of art galleries and a general store with potbellied stove and a definite bias toward the gourmet end of the food chain, the place maintains an authentic feel. Well, it does at least until you enter the very upmarket Pitcher Inn. Once a rustic hostelry frequented by loggers in the 1800s, it burned to the ground in 1993, and recently was rebuilt as a replica of the original. But don't be misled by its columned grace or even the stylish leathery Ralph Lauren look of its reception rooms. Once you see the bedrooms, you'll understand why this place has all the fashionable magazines one-upping each other in florid adjectival syntax.

I had many more enticing back roads to explore in this northern part of the Green Mountains: The narrow track from Lincoln to Jerusalem and onward toward Huntingdon; Highway 17 over the Appalachian Gap from Bristol to Waitsfield; and the rough track south on 32 from Ripton and Goshen.

But stopping by the Pitcher Inn had changed everything. The restaurant now offers an amazing array of food. I decided it was time to take note once again of Frost's admonition about the bear, enjoy a leisurely, delectable dinner, and leave my ramblings until tomorrow. The bear in me smiled and nodded in approval.

TRAVEL NOTES

CLIMATE: Late spring and early fall are ideal times to visit, with the latter offering endless waves of fall-colored mountains.

EASE OF ACCESS: Some local roads are unpaved but well-graded. Back-road travel in winter can be problematic, if not impossible, without a snowmobile.

HIGHLIGHTS: Abundant cultural and other delights in Middlebury, folksy-funk in Bristol, and echoes of Robert Frost (and Norman Rockwell) in the outlying villages. In Middlebury, the Vermont State Craft Center, in an old bobbin mill, has works of Vermont craftspeople.

Costa Rica

MONTEVERDE

The beautiful, near-mythical golden toad
mates in small pools
in Monteverde's cloud forest.

COSTA RICA boasts more than 75 ecologically protected reserves and parks. The Monteverde Cloud Forest Reserve, famous for its range of plant species, wildlife, and a near-mythical golden toad, is one of the most renowned.

Across a narrow landmass bound by the Pacific Ocean and the Caribbean Sea—a three-hour drive from coast to coast at its tightest—nature is abundant and highly diverse. This small Central American nation is the kind of place that all of us, at one time or another, fantasize about visiting—a luxuriously vegetated lost world in a remote highland, far from the tedious trappings of civilization.

No country on Earth has preserved so much of itself in reserves, national parks, and other protected areas. These vary in character from the overpopular Manuel Antonio National Park (a Pacific beach paradise) and Braulio Carrillo National Park (highlighting a volcano hike) to the more serene La Selva Biological Station, Tortuguero National Park (home of endangered turtles), and the strange "dry" tropical forest of Guanacaste National Park in the north.

Nor in any country does the populace more faithfully reflect the peaceful essence of nature. An army does not exist here—a state of grace unique in Latin America, where the military often appears to be an essential component. A country without an army is indeed something to celebrate, as is a nation of policy makers with ecologically sound foresight and convictions. In recent years, practical Costa Rican policies have helped create an ecotourism industry that now surpasses banana and coffee exports as the nation's largest source of foreign exchange.

"But why choose Monteverde?" I was asked by a bunch of newfound "Tico" (Costa Rican) friends in the sprightly little capital of San José. One of them itemized their collective concerns: "First, it's a long hard drive from here, at least four hours, with the last two hours on really rough back roads. Second, they let only 100 people in at any one time. Third, it's expensive, it's wet, it's muddy, the wildlife is hard to see—and the monkeys keep shitting on you!"

"And then," said another, "you still have to drive all the way back!"

"I'm going anyway," I announced with determination. "I'm going because it's the home of the quetzal with all those amazing yard-long tail feathers, the two-toed sloth, and the golden toad, one of the rarest and most beautiful creatures on Earth. Monteverde is a rare

Visitors explore Monteverde's cloud forest.

ecological environment, different from most rain forests on Earth, and, well…," I admitted, "I'm going because I made a reservation at one of the lodges, and it's nonrefundable!"

They nodded and smiled those "well, don't say we never told you" smiles and ordered another round of Imperial beers.

EVER SINCE Carol and David Hughes's photographic forays into this remote part of northwestern Costa Rica, the 31,000-acre Monteverde Cloud Forest Reserve and its profusion of wildlife have become known throughout the world. Naturalists and botanists flock here to lose themselves in the 6,000-foot-high ranges of virgin cloud forest in the Cordillera de Tilarán. They come to study the mating habits of the rare quetzal, to photograph the more than 2,000 native plant species, and to spend weeks high in the jungle canopy examining the world of epiphytes—miniature jungles of plants living on other plants. Nature's appeal is encyclopedic here: 500 species of trees, 100 of mammals, 400 birds, 500 butterflies, 120 reptiles, 50 hummingbirds, 32 bats, 300 orchids, 200 ferns, and to cap it all a number of very elusive cats—puma, jaguar, ocelot, jaguarundi, margay—and more quetzals than anywhere else on Earth.

More than 2,000 native plant species thrive in Monteverde.

But it was the golden toad that really captured my imagination. I had been told that this tiny, beautiful creature can be found only in small pools in the cloud forest, where it comes to mate. Discovered as recently as 1967, the golden toad is unique in color and appearance; indeed, the Monteverde reserve was established in part to protect its habitat. I wanted to see a golden toad for myself.

My doomsayer friends were right about the journey. It *was* long and bone-jarring, and in my spartan automobile, the last 20 miles pummeled my backside to pulp. I finally arrived at dusk to find the dining room of my alpine-looking hotel filled with eager-faced young hikers from Scandinavia singing folk songs, which took me back to my hearty, healthy camping days in the mid-sixties.

AT DAWN, mists filled the lower valleys thousands of feet below, yet the cloud forest reserve on these high ranges was strangely cloud-free, basking in fresh light. I could gaze 40 miles westward to the Pacific across a turbulent, writhing landscape of conical mountains and runty ridges smothered in thick green coats of trees. Billions of them.

I had also been told that sunrise was the best time to set off. So, clutching cameras and a lunch pack—and with a final gaze over the vistas in bleary-eyed awe—I left the soft, early morning sun behind and entered the dark forest.

Within minutes I realized that finding a golden toad would not be easy. Recent storms had made a mire of the signed trail, which wound around fallen trees and thigh-high tangles of roots. Swarms of flies were out early; they seemed to relish the sweat pouring down my face and arms. The stagnant air smelled of

decaying leaves and mossy rot. Occasional views beyond the jungle showed steamy ridges of virgin forest; mists crept higher up the valley sides, and strange rustlings were all around me. Every once in a while came the eerie echoing shrieks of howler monkeys.

After another hour I was a corporeally challenged, mud-caked wreck, flailing up near-vertical hillsides and tumbling down into swampy patches buzzing with cicadas. When the mists came, spreading like tentacles over the forest, everything grew indistinct and blurry in the half-light, creating a mood of fog-bound solitude. Then came a sudden downpour of rain—great gushing gobbets of warm wetness. No one else was around. I lost the trail briefly and felt utterly helpless.

"Struggle is the crucible of character," I reminded myself (a John D. Rockefeller aphorism, I believe), but my mood seemed to suggest otherwise.

Somehow, much later on, I found the pools where golden toads were said to congregate and mate. They were empty—just inky black puddles in the gloom. Disappointed and too tired to walk, I sat among the mossy roots of a fallen tree and let the flies have their way with me. Everything around me seemed so throbbingly alive—almost talking to me. Only sometimes, like this time, I felt stone-deaf.

A couple of elderly ladies laden with binoculars, cameras, and elaborate rain gear—obviously bird-watchers—emerged from the mist and asked if I'd caught a glimpse of one of Monteverde's quetzals.

"No, not yet." I said. "And no golden toads either."

They looked at me in surprise, then at each other.

A latticed walkway disappears into the clouds and forest.

A hummingbird sips nectar from a torch ginger blossom.

"Nobody's told you, then?" one of them asked.

"Told me what?"

"Well, we hate to be the first to let you know, but golden toads haven't been seen here for quite a while. They might even be extinct."

The two women left with apologetic smiles and murmurs of consolation. I continued on a little later, skidding and sliding on the trail, resigned to the fact that I'd more than likely see nothing else but this rampant profusion of forest. If only I'd developed an enthusiasm for epiphytes, I mused. There were countless thousands all about. Or leaf-cutting ants. I'd seen vast, hyperactive chains of them everywhere.

However, all was not lost. Having come across my two ladies again, and peering with them into the green intensity of the forest echoing with rapturous cooings and bell-like birdcalls, I think I saw a sloth. Something was hanging off an epiphyte-smothered branch and moving very slowly, but it seemed to be green.

"Oh, that's only the moss on its fur," said one of the women.

"And they're just too slothful to clean it off!" said the other, delighted by her own pun.

According to my enthusiastic female informants, I spotted a tawny-throated leaf-tosser and a three-wattled bellbird; three odd, wattlelike bits of skin dangled from its throat as it uttered strange metallic boings.

But, no quetzals—no yard-long tail plumes of iridescent emerald green, no bright red breasts, no punkish-looking golden-spiked crowns.

"They're very rare, dear," said one of my ladies (they'd really looked after me since delivering the sad news about the golden toads).

"Don't worry," said the other in a motherly tone. "I'll show you my photographs when we get back."

MUCH (MUCH) later, I staggered back into civilization to be greeted by a middle-aged gentleman in a straw hat carrying two enormous aluminum milk cans. We met by chance near the dairy and small cheese-making plant for which Monteverde is nationally famous. He told me the fascinating story of Monteverde's founding by a group of war-hating Quakers from Alabama, who purchased 6,000 acres in these high hills in the 1950s for a farming community and biological reserve. A portion of the Quakers' original manifesto states, "In contrast to increasing militarism we hope to discover a way of life which will seek the good of each member of the community and to live in a way that will naturally lead to peace in the world rather than war." Their struggles to reach their elusive aerie in oxcarts on almost nonexistent trails, build their own homes, and establish an economically viable colony would, I thought, make a fine movie.

A couple of miles or so farther from here is Santa Elena, a lively village with an abundance of little hotels, its own less well-known cloud forest reserve, and the Children's Eternal Rain Forest, financed with funds raised by schoolchildren from all over the world. Other private reserves and attractions here have expanded in recent years to include Canopy Tour and Skywalk adventures, the Monteverde Butterfly Garden, an Orchid Garden, the Serpentario, and the fascinating Reserva Sendero Tranquilo, where a local family gives informative tours in the rain forest to the growing numbers of tourists who are interested in experiencing such a wealth of biodiversity.

Though it started out forlornly, my adventure had become a fascinating journey through a place that slowly disclosed its chameleon-like character. I learned about the abundance of life in the oddest places.

My Tico friends back in San José have no idea what they're missing up here.

It's a shame about the golden toads, though.

TRAVEL NOTES

CLIMATE: May through November, the rainy season, is the best time to avoid most eco-enthusiasts. **EASE OF ACCESS:** Unless you insist on tackling the long, four-hour drive (half on bad roads) in your own car, it would be best to take a bus from San José to Monteverde. You'll do a lot of walking once you arrive—but if you still decide you'd like transportation, most hotels can arrange for taxis. The reserve entrance is five miles from Santa Elena village. **HIGHLIGHTS:** Exploring one of the Earth's most diverse ecological environments in the reserve, as well as the nature-related attractions outside the reserve.

Bolivia and Peru

LAKE TITICACA

Clouds, dainty as down, float overhead
across an eerie lunar landscape bounded
by the glacier-etched Cordilleras.

IT SEEMED such a miraculous anachronism—a 3,200-square-mile lake in the middle of a vast, wind-scoured Altiplano desert between soaring Andean ranges. More than 900 feet deep in places and set more than 12,000 feet high, Lake Titicaca became a highly revered focal point of ancient cultures, notably the great Inca Empire. At its peak in the 16th century, the Inca civilization encompassed 3,500 miles of the 4,500-mile-long Andean mountain chain. The Incas' worship of the two main Titicaca islands of the Sun and Moon (Sol and Luna) reinforced the isles' importance as tangible expressions of the culture's focal myths—the great legends of the Earth-creators, Manco Capac (Sun) and Mama Ocllo (Moon). To the Incas, this beautiful and lonely lake was the birthplace of their civilization, home of their primary gods, and the nexus of all creation.

After years of curiosity about this place, I was finally sitting silently on the jetty at the Inca Utama Hotel at Huatajata on Titicaca's eastern shore by this fluorescent-blue lake, beneath a condor-speckled sky. Pillow-plump clouds floated overhead across an eerie lunar landscape bounded by the glacier-etched, fang-ridged mountains. I could see a sprinkling of islands

(there are 41 altogether) in the lake hazed in cool morning mists.

I was recovering from the afflictions of soroche (altitude sickness), caused by the oxygen-depleted air, which gave me dizziness, headaches, sleeplessness, and whatnot. But as I drank my third morning cup of mate de coca—a traditional coca-leaf tea with the noxious flavor of diluted mud—I felt better with every sip. Beyond the tiny scattered farms and adobe houses on the lakeshore, I could see a couple of totora fishing boats—constructed, as the pre-Incan Aymara Indians have been doing for centuries, from the long, supple reeds that grow in vast brakes around Titicaca and its islands.

I was feeling very mellow at my hotel. Owned by one of Bolivia's largest and most culturally conscious travel organizations, Crillon Tours, the Inca Utama is a remarkable complex: a spa (coca-cream massages and mud baths), a nighttime observatory for magnificent starscapes and tales of unfamiliar constellations (complete with retractable roof), and three excellent Andean-Altiplano cultural centers.

"We also have a copy of Thor Heyerdahl's great Ra II reed boat here—full size!" said Jorge Jesus Romero Carvajal, manager of the hotel.

An Aymara woman sells woven tapestries near Lake Titicaca.

A stone archway frames Titicaca, the world's highest, large navigable lake.

"He is the great Kon-Tiki man. He used the reeds and many men from the lake to build it. He made Titicaca famous."

The following day, with a small group of fellow travelers, I departed from the hotel to the islands of the Sun and Moon. As one might expect, legends abound here—tales of a sunken city, lost treasure, a Loch Ness-like aquatic creature (Titty!), and giant two-foot-long frogs. The frogs, first discovered by Jacques Cousteau, are no legend—I ate two enormous and delicious legs in one sitting, along with a *conechocuis* (roasted guinea pig) at a lakeside restaurant—yes, both tasted like chicken.

After an hour of surging westward across the choppy lake beneath pearly swirls of high cirrus clouds, the hydrofoil docked for 20 minutes or so at the islet of La Luna.

Navigating Titicaca

I wandered off to explore the most substantial (if rather ragged) ruins on the lake. I had seen it described variously as an Incan nunnery for the *Virgenes del Sol* (Virgins of the Sun), as a harem, and as a home for sacrificial virgins. It may even have served as all three, at one time or another.

The next hydrofoil stop was Isla del Sol, five miles west of Isla de la Luna. The schedule allowed only a one-hour stop, but on a whim I decided to spend a night here. It seemed stupid to come all this way to Titicaca just for a fun-filled, rush-rush, day-long boat trip.

Eager to feel the spirit of this legendary place, I left the other travelers at the southern end of the two-by-seven-mile island. The climb up the island's mountainous spine was laborious. Making it even worse was the fact of my exposure to the scorching sun, merciless at this altitude of almost 13,000 feet. The initial part of the ascent scales 210 footworn stone steps, which lead from the beach to the famous Fuente del Inca—the water source the Spanish so desperately wanted to believe was the Fountain of Youth. A single swallow from each of the fountain's three cascades of ice-cold spring water, I had been told, was guaranteed to rejuvenate me by at least ten years. So I sampled each one—and then, for good luck, drank a few mugfuls.

I'm still waiting for the effects to kick in.

Posada del Inca, near the ridge-top village of Yumani, was "just a little farther, Señor, not even to the top of the hill." My informant was an elderly man in a heavy poncho and brightly colored *chullo* (a long wool cap with tasseled earflaps). Off I set at a dazzling pace, climbing more rough steps that wriggled between ancient Inca-created terraces.

I lost count of the steps after 400. Everybody and everything had passed me by, including diminutive Aymara women in traditional attire (originally decreed by the Spanish conquistadors to reflect Spanish dress back home): a felt bowler hat over coal-black, centrally parted and often-pigtailed hair, a *chompa* (sweater), multi-layered petticoats and skirts, a cloak, and multicolored backpacks. They energetically ascended the seemingly endless steps, along with llamas, golden-skinned pigs, bleary-eyed donkeys, and chattering gaggles of school kids invariably asking this worn-out stranger for "*caramellos, por favor.*"

Tottering with tiredness, I entered the posada gates by the side of a tiny Catholic church with a tower precariously atilt. The place was no five-star resort, but the food was solid—thick vegetable soups, sautéed lake trout, lots of mate de coca—and the chilly nights were relieved by a warm stove and rubber hot-water bottles. Before retiring, in the company of sighing breezes I sat on the patio overlooking the eastern slopes of the islands, enjoying magnificent moonlit vistas over snow-sheened mountains, a silvered lake, and distant ghostly islets beneath a nightscape of incredible star patterns billowing across the blackness.

ISLA DEL SOL has great walking trails, particularly to the Inca ruins at its northern tip, but I decided to enjoy the peace of the posada and sketch the Aymara charms of Yumani village. Then, before mellow leisure slid into lethargic laziness, I descended those interminable steps and caught a boat. After a bouncy ride that lasted 20 rollicking minutes, we entered the calm bay of Copacabana, which struck me as a roaring metropolis after my quiet time on Isla del Sol. From the dock stretched a curve of beach stroked by soft surf and dotted with boats, kayaks, donkeys, colorful *tricolas* (tricycles—a local form of taxi), and countless tiny snack bars offering barbecued trout, pork, *pejerrey* (a delicious white lake fish), and roasted chicken. I could see the impressive domed towers of the gleaming white Spanish-Moorish cathedral adorned in colorful tiles.

I set off up the long hill to the ornately landscaped plaza to give thanks at the Moorish-flavored shrine of the Dark Virgin of the Lake (Virgen de Candelaria), a focal point of national miracle-healing pilgrimages.

I had been intending to stay longer in this lively little town, but a group of Australian backpackers persuaded me to join them in a bus heading for the ancient remains of the city of Tiwanacu, set in a vast desert plain at the southern end of the lake. Here I had to completely revise my concept of the history of this region.

A young Bolivian woman I met by chance, told me with exuberant pride that "the culture here of the Aymara Indians is at least 2,000 years older than the Inca's culture." Although the remains of temples and pyramids are somewhat meager, the bold, confident styling of the statuary and great carved gates were uniquely impressive.

Titicaca, I told her, was beginning to feel onionlike to me—layer upon layer of history, civilization, and meaning.

"Oh yes!" she laughed, "Just like life!"

TRAVEL NOTES

CLIMATE: Temperatures are remarkably even at around 65° F to 75° F year-round; November to March can be rainy.

EASE OF ACCESS: It's less than an hour's drive by car to Lake Titicaca from La Paz or its airport. Once at the lake, numerous tour companies offer hydrofoil, catamaran, and other boat tours to the islands.

HIGHLIGHTS: The islands of Lake Titicaca; the Andean Roots museum and the exhibition complex at the Inca Utama hotel, which provide an excellent introduction to the region's history and culture.

Chile

ATACAMA DESERT

The towering Andean spine of snowcapped mountains and volcanic cones rises as a huge, hazy wall.

HAVING JUST driven the 60 or so miles southeast from the town of Calama, high above the dry and unpeopled northern Chilean coast, to the adobe-built desert town of San Pedro de Atacama, I hadn't expected to come face to face with "Miss Chile." There was something in the delicate elongated shape of her face, her narrow, bony shoulders, and long dark tresses of hair that suggested vulnerability. I felt she was possibly shy, but fun to flirt with. There was just one tiny problem. She was dead.

Very dead. Eight thousand years dead actually, and thoroughly eviscerated, folded, and packed into an earthen pit in a waterless desert from which she emerged this century a little thinner, bonier, but with hair still neatly plaited and her mouth curled in a toothy half-smile.

There she was, in a remote oasis village at the foot of 19,455-foot-high Licancábur volcanic cone, sitting in a prominent display case in one of Chile's most intriguing museums—the Archeological Museum of Father Gustave Le Paige. The vast collection of artifacts in the Jesuit priest's museum tells the 10,000-year history of the Atacameño culture and its incorporation into the Inca Empire in the 15th century as the conquerors spread south

from Peru along the famed Inca Road. Subsequent depredation of the culture by Pedro de Valdivia and the Spanish conquistadors in the mid-1500s led to the destruction of the Atacameños' fortified villages—the pukarás—and the establishment of a strict system of serfdom controlled from such ancient communities as San Pedro de Atacama.

The discovery of vast nitrate and copper deposits during the 20th century, in the desert region closer to the coast, brought a brief boom-town era to San Pedro when it became a major stop on the lucrative cattle trail from the Argentinean borderlands to the burgeoning new mining towns. Today things are a little quieter, although San Pedro's reputation as a way station on the "gringo trail" (a favorite route of Western backpackers over the Andes to Bolivia, Peru, and Argentina) ensures that its ancient Atacameño origins will enjoy yet one more reincarnation. I'd like to think that coquettish "Miss Chile"—immortalized in her display case—is pleased by all the unexpected attention.

The compact little Hispanic-flavored community of fewer than 2,000 residents is a place of sun-bleached adobe walls, narrow shadowy streets, and a plaza that invites you to sit for

It has been more than 50 years since the parched Atacama has seen rain.

A man passes by a Catholic church in San Pedro de Atacama.

hours. (You'll do plenty of sitting under the pepper trees by the old whitewashed Spanish church.) You're a heady 8,000 feet high here; the desert eases out in a broad, treeless vastness. The towering Andean spine of snowcapped mountains and volcanic cones rises as a huge hazy wall in the east—beautiful, dramatic, but oddly aloof.

Deserts and their dreamlike immensity are best experienced alone. I love their aura of infinite nowhereness, which makes you feel you're on the farthest margins of things familiar. I rejoice in their colors—the rich morning blendings of orange with beige, gold with brilliant silver, brick red against white, burnished gold streaked with amber. After noon comes the flat time, with its thick intoxicating heat and dancing mirages, when colors merge and become a dun, hammered hue and the land is leached of form and edges. The Atacama—a desert of eye-scouring aridity and brittle, cadaverous ridges and scarps—is particularly unusual: Parts of it go without measurable rainfall for decades, yet it bursts into a sudden flowery bloom every spring.

The Atacama is also a place of strange salt lakes. One of them, the Salar de Atacama in the 30,000-acre Reserva Nacional Los Flamencos, is populated by hundreds of pink flamingos. Here, ancient stone and adobe villages suddenly pop out of the shimmering vastness or snuggle deep in almost invisible canyons around oases. Out of the dramatically dry and eroded Valley of the Moon, near San Pedro, appears an unearthly array of monster-like mountains, bizarre rock formations, and huge black-sand dunes smoothed by the hot desert winds of this embalmed land.

Then there's the most popular place of all—the geysers in El Tatio, 60 miles or so north of San Pedro. This geological anomaly was one of the main reasons for my visit—only no one told me that I'd have to leave my lodging at the bone-chilling hour of three a.m.

I'd become rather fond of this little town with its funky, nirvana-seeking backpackers; its narrow lanes laced with oleanders, hollyhocks, and roses; its tiny restaurants offering inexpensive platters of steak, chicken-filled empanadas (crisp pastry delights served with pebre, or salsa), hearty Spanish cazuela (a stew of potato or corn and chicken or beef), and pastel de choclo (a corn, raisin, and chicken pie).

It was refreshing to spend time with the young Earth gypsies who congregated in the plaza by the church and hear their travel tales and the nonchalant, devil-may-care way in which they described their individual journeys along the gringo trail. Almost without exception they had sloughed off for a while their past and future lives seeming to enjoy that blissful state of "nowness" advocated by gurus and New Age-philosophers but rarely experienced by most career and ambition-driven individuals. One young man from Denmark with long blonde hair, sapphire blue eyes, and a smile of utter contentment, suggested that he recognized the challenges that lay ahead in his "serious life" but for the moment he just wanted to explore "outwardly and inwardly."

BUT I HAD to leave. It was essential—so I'd been told—to reach the geysers before dawn to experience their strange charms. This explains why I bid a reluctant farewell to this enticing oasis in a freezing predawn where a ghostly frost coated palm fronds after a derangingly hot,

100° F day. I clattered across the desert in a rented jeep, switchbacking over ridges on a rough corrugated track that seemed determined to shake every tooth out of my head and pummel my brain into gooey mush.

Twice I almost rolled off the track on sneaky hairpin bends over the 13,000-foot-high Las Vizcachas pass. But finally, after two hours in brilliant moonlight beneath a night sky crackling with stars, I coasted into an eerie mountain bowl set at a soroche (altitude sickness)–stimulating height of 14,173 feet. Surrounded by soaring snowcapped Andean peaks, I found myself in the mile-wide fumarole field, curling wraiths of steam rising—in some cases hundreds of feet high—from dozens of active blowholes.

Walking was treacherous in the bone-chilling half-light; some of the boiling pools were barely more than a yard across and hardly visible in the steam clouds. I had no desire for scalded legs or worse, so I kept to the fringes of the field, listening to its seething and bubbling. Some of the larger geysers burst in great sprays from altar-size encrustations of lime and minerals; more insidious were the burping, bubbling, or bursting chocolaty mudholes within deep, dark recesses edged by moss.

The first sear of light came from between two huge mountains and transformed the gray lumpish hillside behind me into a golden cascade of eroded scarps and crevices covered in brush-stroke flecks of paja brava grasses. The billowing steam columns glowed and sparkled. Other visitors had arrived and cameras clicked all around me. Then a cheer went up as the sun broke through a cleft and warmth began to permeate the bowl. A handful of Andean geese stretched their broad wings and cute little

Otherworldly formations create the Atacama's Valley of the Moon.

squirrel-like vizcachas preened on the slopes above the steaming pools.

From the far side of the bowl came shrieks of delight. I scampered between blowholes to see what was happening. Six backpackers were gaily throwing off their clothes and leaping naked into a natural hot pool. Nearby the highest geyser of all hurled its boiling fury into a steam column more than 300 feet high.

As the sun rose, the steam began to lose its condensation fury in the warming air, and the columns diminished under an increasingly brilliant blue sky. It was time to move on in search of the elusive Indian villages I'd heard were hidden in the vast desert below.

The track was even worse than before. I negotiated my jeep down the long scrub-covered slopes, dotted with occasional clusters of wild llama-like vicuña and alpaca, to a seemingly endless plateau of gravel and broken stones. It was flat, featureless, and immense, scorched into vibrant bronze streaks by an endlessly searing sun. There can't possibly be a village around here, I thought as I scoured the desolation.

But I was wrong.

An hour or so after I had left the geysers, the desert suddenly broke open, revealing the deep gash of a canyon. I stood on the rim and peered down. There, way below me, glimmered a winding stream glinting silver in the sun, brilliant-green strips of terraced fields, and clusters of flamelike Lombardy poplars, golden with early fall colors. I could see a tiny white church on top of a sheer-walled bluff and a village of thick-walled stone houses along the stream. I had found the elusive and ancient community of Caspaña, set like some Chilean Brigadoon deep in a hidden green canyon and rich in Atacameño culture.

Enchantment grew as I explored the village, admiring the enormity of its stone walls and terraces. I smiled—and was smiled back at by stony-faced women in long skirts and bowler-type hats—as I climbed the steep, stone-paved streets to the old village, perched atop cliffs in the traditional manner of ancient Chilean fortress villages.

As I wandered its narrow streets, past adobe homes and courtyards, I could feel the peace and slow rhythms of this secretive place seducing me. "You could live here awhile," whispered that temptress in my brain once again. Apparently not, for within a few hours I was back in the jeep and careering once again on corrugated desert tracks in search of a second, equally elusive village set in its own hidden canyon near the confluence of the Salado and Loa Rivers.

Founded by the Spanish conquistadors, Chiuchiu is set on the ancient Inca Road near one of the Atacama's oddest anomalies, a half-mile-wide lagoon of crystalline water more than 450 feet deep. Today stone and adobe houses line the main street and narrow alleys. At the center, bounded by the Loa River on one side and a recently restored plaza on the other, sits one of Chile's most beloved native monuments: Chiuchiu's Church of San Francisco. This amazingly massive whitewashed structure supported by numerous huge buttresses was built in 1675 with walls more than five feet thick.

I knew I'd be back in Calama later in the day, nestled in air-conditioned comfort at my hotel and tucking into some lavish dinner washed down with margarita-like pisco sours and elegant Chilean wines. For the moment, though, I preferred to remain in the cool shadows of the church, watching vulture-like jotes circle in the blue sky and llamas snoozing by the river below, and enjoying the aroma of baking bread emanating from a domed adobe oven beside a tiny farmstead nestled at the base of the high canyon walls.

The seductions of civilization could wait. In this region that clings tenaciously to its secrets, I sat quietly in the sumptuous silence, feeling the warm desert wind on my face.

TRAVEL NOTES

CLIMATE: Unexpectedly balmy for a desert, with year-round day temperatures from the upper 70s to the upper 80s during December through May; June through September nights can be chilly and even ice-cold in the Southern Hemisphere winter. Sunscreen and layered clothing are essential. **EASE OF ACCESS:** After a two-hour flight from Santiago to Calama, it is a 60-mile bus or car ride on a good road to San Pedro. If you prefer to avoid do-it-yourself desert driving, there are plenty of organized tours running out of Calama. **HIGHLIGHTS:** Ancient desert communities, soaring volcanoes, salt lakes, protected colonies of pink flamingos, and spuming geysers. A luxury desert resort, if you're in the mood for extravagant splurges.

France

PYRENEES-BASQUE AREA

The Pyrenees range is home to
the Basque people whose culture is so
ancient that its origins are unknown.

IT WAS in Bayonne, the lively seacoast city and gateway to the Basque country of southwest France, that I saw a crudely painted sign on a wall: EUSKARA: ZAZPIAK BAT: The Land of the Basque! The Seven Provinces Are One!"

"I think a Spaniard painted that," said a young man standing nearby. "They've always wanted their own country."

I asked if he considered himself first a Frenchman or a Basque. He didn't hesitate.

"Oh, I'm a Basque first, of course. Always."

The territory of the Basques, in the western Pyrenees of France, continuing on the other side of the mountains and along the northern coast in Spain, is the setting for a great cultural mystery. Its residents are of obscure racial and linguistic origin, nationalistic and proud. Although the roots of their civilization are unclear—theorists have claimed links with everything from Amazon tribes to the lost continent of Atlantis, and, most credibly, a Celtic tribe known as the Vascones—the Basque people are nonetheless extensive and characterized by strong ethnic identity.

In a tiny village about 20 miles southwest of the town of Pau, in the foothills of the Pyrenees, I walked down a lane to a cluster of whitewashed farmhouses. Snuggled in its tight valley beneath sculpted canopies of cumulus clouds, the village was silent. Its barnlike houses—trimmed with oxblood-colored shutters and hunched under heavy pantile roofs—stood around a small, unpaved square. A sign on a farmyard gate advertised FROMAGE DÉGUSTATION—SE VENDE: A tasting first, followed by a purchase if the cheese lived up to expectations.

I knocked on an enormous wooden door that absorbed the sound and stung my knuckles. Then I noticed the brass knocker, and gave that a hearty clout. The door opened slowly, revealing the ruddy face of a woman dressed in a blue pinafore. She motioned me inside and immediately shut the door behind. After the bright sunlight, I found it hard to see anything at all and walked straight into the corner of a thick wooden table.

She asked if I had hurt my leg on the table; I congratulated her on its sturdiness. Then she reached for a carving knife big enough to behead a bull, sliced off a healthy sample of sheep's milk cheese from a golden-crusted wheel, and offered it to me. I bit into it and let it rest in my mouth while it softened and turned to pungent creaminess.

Cattle rest at the base of the Pyrenees Mountains in France.

A Basque man sports the traditional black beret.

Much later, after an extensive series of tastings, I selected half a wheel of a three-month-old beauty, the skin crusted with pale green mold, the fresh flesh delicate as a peach.

EARLIER THAT morning I had been the sole witness of dawn from the Boulevard des Pyrénées in Pau. This proud and elegant ancient city, center of Protestantism and birthplace of King Henri of Navarre, smacks of the indulgence of wealth. Warm winters have for generations attracted indolent and infirm Britishers to lavish aeries in the apartments along the boulevard. Elegant cafés, fine dress shops, and revered restaurants in the old town satisfy the refined tastes of well-heeled convalescents from all parts of Europe. In daily ritual, they promenade along the boulevard in the shadows of Chateau de Pau to the elegant casino.

But at dawn, the city is silent.

The first shaft of gold strikes the white peaks of the Pyrenees with an almost audible resonance and bathes the whole writhing range of peaks, crevasses, arêtes, and cols in a brilliant fanfare of light and shadow. There's only one problem: When leaving Pau, traveling southwest toward the Soule and Basque country, the glowing mountains are often lost behind the turbulent contours of the foothills. At Oloron-Ste.-Marie, a charming little market town with its fortresslike church of Ste.-Croix, the peaks are still visible, but farther along past Aramits there are long stretches when they disappear altogether.

Whereas Pau greets the mountains wide-eyed and open-mouthed, Tardets turns its back on them and clusters tightly around its arcaded main square. Posters in the Basque language, full of the letters "E" and "X", are plastered on peeling walls. Unlike the more authentic Basque towns of the Labourd region to the west—characterized by red pantile roofs, whitewashed walls, red or green shutters, and traditional farmhouse-style homes—Soule towns possess delicate, double-pitched roofs of gray stone or slate, thick walls built of river rocks occasionally stuccoed and painted, and churches with three-pointed belfries.

The road from the alpine pastures down the valley toward St. Étienne de Baïgorry passes through a number of tough Basque villages, with their groupings of church, cemetery, town hall (herriko etxea), inn, and the ubiquitous fronton court, home of pelota and a dozen other unique Basque ball games. Most famous is the lightning-speed jai alai, using hooked chistera baskets, but the locals also play mainnue (using the hand to hit the ball), gant (the same idea, but with leather gloves), pala (using rounded sticks), and sare (with tennis racquet–shaped bats). The larger towns often boast their own trinquet, an enclosed court that is most popular during the cold winter months.

Sometimes the court occupies a major part of the main street, and if a game is in progress, traffic must wait for the end of the round. In other towns, such as Mauléon, the court doubles as the town square. In Aïnhoa, a classic and beautiful bastide town bursting with traditional

Basque architecture, the church allows its south wall to be used for the game.

These games are far more than idle pastimes; they're part of the ritual of Basque community. Reputations lasting a lifetime are made and broken on the courts. Each evening, when the young men of the village begin their rounds of mainnue, the elders in their jute-soled espadrilles and floppy berets gather in a group like somber black ravens and watch every move and nuance of play. At the end of each round they huddle together, mumbling in their ancient Euskara language full of guttural clicks and pauses that sound like recorded voices played at half-speed, backward. Billows of smoke emerge from a chimney of beret-topped, cigarette-puffing heads as they discuss the quality of play and the excellence or otherwise of local youths.

In a memorable 40-mile, picture-postcard loop drive that passed through the historic and authentically Basque towns of Ascain, Sare, Aïnhoa, and St.-Étienne, I arrived in St.-Jean-Pied-de-Port. Once an important stopping place on the great international pilgrimage route to Santiago de Compostela in Spain's Galicia region, St.-Jean is also the northern gateway to the legendary Pass of Roncesvalles. This is the hub of the French Basque territory. The narrow main street, approached through boldly towered ramparts, climbs steeply up toward the 17th-century Citadelle circling the rock-pocked hill above the town. The houses, in the traditional Basque colors of red and white, form a continuous swath of shutters and dark windows on both sides of the street. Headstones over most of the doors record in boldly chiseled letters the date of construction and the name of the builders. Some have optimistic mottoes—"Peace is on this house"—while others are more morose: "Remember Death!" A crunched dwelling with a wood-frame structure and wide overhanging roof is dated 1510, and many of the others were built in the 1600s.

For a town that enjoys an active summer season, St.-Jean-Pied-de-Port is remarkably unspoiled. Most of the shops and stalls are clustered around the church at the lower end of the main street. Only a handful of visitors manage the long haul up the cobblestone path to the massive Citadelle, to perch on a wall with views over the town and valley and broad vistas of the Pyrenees. Tiny gardens are filled with vegetables and the inevitable collection of hens and lone goats munching on piles of hay. There are few flowers; the land is too valuable and normally used only for growing the basic necessities. As one Basque told me with an air of disdain: "You can always tell the Basques who've been living abroad. They fill their gardens with flowers and buy their vegetables somewhere else."

Traditional ox cart

BASQUES TEND to be private people and don't take to strangers; outsiders are frequently seen as irritating, camera-clicking intruders, always looking for a bit of instant folklore to snap up and take home. So I was fortunate in St.-Jean to get to know a Basque family.

My benefactor was a half-Basque pharmacist I'd met, who generously took me to visit her relatives on a farm a few miles outside the town.

"We will go together. You'll see how people live out here."

We paused first at a plain church that seemed to grow out of the adjoining stone barns, and squeezed in through a tiny door. I looked up, amazed. Rustically crude on the outside, the interior contained three tiers of intricately carved balconies stretching around the back wall and the two nave walls. As my eyes grew accustomed to the dark, I noticed it was adorned with elaborate frescoes, panels, pillars, arches, angels, and Madonnas, all mingled with hexagonal shapes in bright circles.

I later visited a score of churches in the Basque country, and each one contained two or three levels of balconies, painted walls, and hugely ornate altars, which seemed to be pushing the walls out with their exuberance. Many churches feature ancient discoidal headstones, crudely carved with names, dates (many pre-13th century), and Celtic designs, and inscribed with Basque names—La Famille Tafernaberria, La Famille Gelehetaburia, and La Famille Aitzineko-Borda.

We finally arrived at the farm and she led the way through the now familiar barnlike doors, into the broad main hall. This, according to my guide, was a typical Basque farmhouse. "It's true. In some of the poorer farms the main part is still used as the storage place when there is no separate barn. The stairs lead to the two upper levels and the doors go to separate rooms. Usually mother and father and grandparents live downstairs and the children upstairs. When the eldest son marries, he either builds another house nearby or also lives upstairs with his wife, and perhaps even children. In the Basque family the farm goes to the eldest son or daughter. The others have to leave and marry into another farm or—so many times—go abroad, usually to America. In America they are often shepherds, or work in restaurants. They often make enough money to come home and build their own homes. Why do you think there's so much building going on in the valleys? They're all coming home!"

Outside, the carved eaves, painted dark red, projected three feet beyond the white wall. Immediately below was a balcony, sheltered by the eaves, from which dangled hundreds of drying peppers and pimientos (essential elements of Basque cuisine). At ground level, a sheltered strip of land, the itchasura, was planted with laurel trees. To many Basque families, this plot is regarded as sacred, and stillborn children are often traditionally buried here instead of the family plot at the cemetery.

After a protracted session sipping izarra, a pungent Basque liqueur flavored with the essence of Pyrenean flowers, I sat down with the rest of the family to enjoy what seemed like an endless dinner—soups, pâtés, cheeses, meat pies, an enormous pot-au-feu (beef casserole), and bottle after bottle of strong local wine. Afterward, as we sat talking on benches around the open fire in the dining room, I thanked the farmer and his wife for the hospitality. "Oh, this is nothing. Go to my brother's restaurant sometime. It's in the hills. It's not a tourist place. He will feed you until you must beg him to stop.

Isn't that so?" the farmer asked, turning to my pharmacist friend.

She laughed and nodded. "The meals in our country places go on forever. It's one of our favorite traditions!"

Over the following days I began to understand why the Basques are so proud of their unique traditions and ancient culture, and why they consider themselves a separate ethnic group in European society. Initial modest demands for semi-autonomy, particularly from the Spanish Basque region on the south side of the Pyrenees, have been lost in the tumult of regional insurrection. The French Basque region remains tranquil, but there is something so deeply independent in the Basque soul that one wonders if the desire for a separate nation will ever cease. And I'll always remember that Frenchman's remark in Bayonne: "Oh, I'm a Basque first, of course. Always."

TRAVEL NOTES

CLIMATE: Almost any time except winter is ideal for exploring the French Basque country, although summers, particularly August, can be a little hot and hectic in the more touristy coastal centers.

EASE OF ACCESS: Bayonne, Biarritz, St.-Jean-de-Luz, and Pau are all easy to reach by car or bus and are excellent bases from which to begin explorations. An appealing option is a 500-mile drive south from Paris, passing through Cognac, the Bordeaux wine country, the western Périgord region, and Armagnac.

HIGHLIGHTS: The fabulous high Pyrenees scenery, the unique Soule/Labourdin Basque architecture, frantic pelota games.

Morocco

ATLAS MOUNTAINS

The real adventure is crossing the High Atlas Mountains and exploring the plains on the Saharan fringe.

"BISM'ALLAH—In the name of God."

For a moment there is total silence.

Inside a mud house, we pause and whisper the ritual grace before tea is served from a battered tin teapot. The room is black; my eyes are still blinded by the brilliance of the desert outside. The tea splatters in small glasses; my senses fill with the aroma of steeped mint, the sheepy smell of *babouche* slippers and djellabas (thick, hooded kaftans), the purr of a cat close by, the soft chatter of women outside, within the high-walled courtyard.

This is the way to do it, I told myself.

I'd avoided all the guided coach tours from Marrakech, and reluctantly decided against visiting the famed Merzouga dunes south of Erfoud and the awesome Todra Gorge near Tinerhin (both south of the High Atlas Mountains) due to the recent overcommercialization and excessive prices. I had a few spare days, so I hired a car with a readiness to let things just happen—which is how I came to be sitting on a coarse Moroccan carpet in this adobe home with Ahmed and his brother, enjoyably sipping sweet mint tea.

I'd finally torn myself away from the tantalizations of Marrakech—its dark, mysterious souks and the fierce, frenzied intensity of its Djemaa el-Fna marketplace. I soared out of the city, up the tight curves of the High Atlas, toward the Tizi N'Tichka Pass (7,415 feet), along ocher fortified villages bound by high mud walls, and ultimately reached the fringes of the Sahara. Views over alarming precipices revealed villagers tending narrow terrace plots of wheat and barley. Soon I was deep in the wild domain of the Lords of Atlas, fierce Berber chieftains who once ruled these lofty realms and repelled all invaders well into this century. The *Imazighen* ("Free People of the Land"), as the Berbers call themselves, have inhabited Morocco for well over 2,000 years. These tribal people have arduously survived the waves of cultural influence imposed by the Phoenicians, Romans, Arabs, Black Africans, Portuguese, Spanish, and most recently, the French. France adopted Morocco as a protectorate from 1912 to 1956 and still failed to subdue the Imazighen in what is also called *biladal siba*—"land of dissidence."

Today in this peaceful country of around 30 million, the Berber region remains an aloof but alluring bastion. It feels like a place where traditions die hard and the old ways are very much in place among the snow-clad peaks.

In only moments, direct sun will bake the vast Sahara.

I MET Ahmed at a roadside café where I'd just enjoyed a lunch of thick *harira*, a rich meat broth with chickpeas and lentils served with dates and lemon slices flecked with cinnamon. He asked for a lift to his family village over the pass (hitchhiking is very common in Morocco) and presented me a piece of Atlas geode as a goodwill gesture. He spoke passable English and made a lively companion as we zigzagged down the southern slopes of the mountains, passing young boys holding ferocious-looking lizards by horny tails and rickety roadside stands selling chunks of sparkling Atlas quartzite.

We suddenly left behind the green terraces and flurries of cedars. Scrawny bushes seemed to exist on sufferance and little else. Villages were stacked tightly, almost invisible in clefts, scratching a living from tiny oases of date palms and barley. Buzzards soared on the thermals, watching for flickers of life among the rocks; a bloody-beaked eagle stood its ground, talons impaled in something extremely dead and messy on the road in front of my laboring Renault 4, known affectionately here as the Moroccan Mulc.

The pause at Ahmed's house was welcome. The simple setting in which he and his family lived seemed a reflection of the land itself—powerful, even majestic in its lack of superfluous detail. Outside the mountains soared abruptly from shadowy canyons. Inside the house a thought occurred to me: True freedom

A young girl plays in a Berber village in Morocco.

Clouds hover above the Atlas Mountains that border Marrakech.

is knowing your real needs and smiling at how simple they are.

I could have stayed, but I was impatient for the Sahara. I wanted to see and sense the thrill of a space that sweeps 2,000 miles into the heart of Africa. I had hoped Morocco would let me experience Africa, but Africa is too big, too complex, too grand a scale for the mind to encompass at once. Like trying to think of the universe.

Swooping south through vertiginous gorges and across sawdust-colored foothills, I finally arrived at a place where the plains stretched out to nothingness; not exactly the Sahara, but an enticing foretaste. I paused at the picture-book hilltop town of Tifoultout, once a stately palace of El Glaoui, Pasha of Marrakech, and now an impressive pile of towering adobe walls and labyrinthine alleys skittering down to a dry riverbed, bronzed in the afternoon sun and wrapped in silence. A couple of dogs barked and nothing else.

I was about 120 miles southeast of Marrakech when I drove into the town of Ouarzazate. It was one big red yawn—dead, hot, dull—so I scampered off across the broad, rock-littered plains, a scarlet-ocher Martian landscape. An abrupt range of black obsidian hills, gashed with canyons, gleamed like glass. A Saharan wind, the hot *sergi*, blew fiercely, and the sand cut my face like a thousand tiny stilettos.

The following day, in intoxicating desert heat, I paused in Agdz, a hectic hilltop town with a main square full of Moroccan carpets and "antique" Berber jewelry. Then I slipped slowly down into the oases of the Drâa Valley. All around were dry, shattered crags and buttes, but alongside the meandering river was a veritable jungle of date palms and almond and orange orchards, set among green carpets of barley and alfalfa. The Drâa inhabitants are different from mountain Berber tribes. Many Drawa are black, descendants of slaves brought north generations ago by Saharan nomads. The men have shaved heads bound by white turbans; the women shroud themselves in black dresses and shawls trimmed with thin strips of brightly colored ribbon and silver trinkets. The veil is an imperative here: The women fold up like bats if they suspect the presence of an outsider. They have an almost telepathic sensitivity to approaching foreigners and hate being photographed.

The ksour here are straight out of the *Arabian Nights*, with high, square towers and crumbling, turreted, red mud walls, slits for windows, and six-inch-thick slabs of wood for doors. The women gather around communal wells, constantly conversing; the men discuss their affairs in dusty groups of seemingly insensate dormancy; children scamper everywhere.

Around 130 miles to the southeast of Ouarzazate, Zagora was almost as dull. But now I could finally sense the Sahara. Horizons flattened and sand devils swirled across the plains. I wanted dunes and camels and the "Blue People"—Tuareg nomads dressed in indigo-dyed djellabas that have stained their skins blue. Their faces were in the picture I carried in my expectant mind when I thought of the Sahara.

A young guide sensed my despondency and led me through a fortified village south of town, along a mile of sandy lanes enclosed by mud walls and high bamboo fences and—finally—to dunes! Miles and miles of them stretched in golden glory to hazy mountain horizons. I thanked him and set off to exorcise my Lawrence of Arabia fantasies under a still-burning sun.

At last I had arrived somewhere—or, more precisely, nowhere. This sense of Saharan infinity had brought me all the way from Marrakech in my rattle-trap Renault. Wandering across this strange, enticing landscape, swimming in light, I had the strangest urge to keep wandering, to lose myself in the folds of the dunes, to vanish. Perhaps I would emerge somewhere else much later, a completely changed creature.

A sense of timelessness began to creep in. I saw spectacular mirages where the whole landscape became a lake-studded panorama of blue and gold. Eventually I found shade in the lee of a dune and watched the day slowly fade into a fireball in the breathless still of evening. For a few magical minutes everything became a brilliant scarlet—the sand, the sky, and me—and then just as quickly the color leeched away, leaving a strange dead grayness and a chill in the evening breeze.

By the time I had retraced my steps to the ksar, it was dark and the stars were out by the billion, strewn across a velvet-black dome. I felt enervated. I had touched the desert and it had touched me in return.

TRAVEL NOTES

CLIMATE: Cooler seasons—March to May and October to December. Summer temperatures reach above 100° F.

EASE OF ACCESS: Atlas pass roads, some of which exceed 6,500 feet, are a test of driving skills and engine endurance.

HIGHLIGHTS: Dramatic mountainscapes, tightly packed mud villages, colorful markets, and Morocco's rich *tagine* stews.

India

JAISALMER

There's nothing but the vast desert...
then, the golden mirage of an ancient
fortress city emerges.

DRIVING MORE than five hours from Jodhpur, across miles of Rajasthan's scorching Thar Desert, I'd become accustomed to the barren monotony of burned plains. The Indian landscape is always large. Scenery changes slowly here, and time flows seamlessly. There are few surprises. It's not boring, though. It's a pleasant kind of mind-numbing neutrality; the brain switches off and you're left with a floating sensation similar, in some ways, to deep meditation.

So for a long time, there was nothing. Then suddenly something—a vague blur on the horizon slowly taking form. It could have been a dust cloud, or an isolated butte eroding into the interminably sandy plain. But the shadings were too evenly spaced. Surely those were walls and towers I could see—a castle, a fortress, a Tolkienesque fantasy? The road was heading straight for it.

A few houses appeared to my left—poor mud-walled places with conical roofs and dusty compounds bound by fences of cactus and piled sagebrush. I passed a raggedy line of old men carrying huge bundles of twigs on their heads like enormous, comic hats; goats and children frolicking in the yellow dust; and dusky-eyed women, some with massive clay water pots balanced atop their intricately plaited hair, moving slowly and sensually in bright red saris and ornately embroidered vests. I heard the rasp of sun-shriveled stalks and brittle grasses waving in the hot desert breeze. The ocher blur on the horizon began to take shape. It had a crenelated and buttressed profile like a fortress. But it was far too big.

It was Jaisalmer, ancient enclave of the Rawals of western Rajasthan. Standing alone in this vast wilderness, the city is a golden fantasy—one of India's most romantic and unspoiled hidden places. A two- or three-day camel ride east from the Pakistan border across the dune-striated Thar Desert, Jaisalmer is a golden stone mirage. Spread across a rocky hill and bound by battlements and unbroken walls more than 200 feet high in places, it resembles an Indian version of France's walled city of Carcassonne, or maybe something out of the *Arabian Nights* sagas—or one of the finest sand castles you'll ever see.

YOU ENTER another realm here. Rajasthan has always been considered a place apart in Indian history, reinforced by its isolation amid arid

A Haveli facade reflects the sun in Rajasthan, India.

western deserts. Evidence of civilizations here have been traced back to 2500 B.C., but recorded history really began with the tribal republics and warrior clans of the sixth century A.D., the most powerful of which were led by the fierce Bhatti Rajputs. They were constantly at war with one another, though in later centuries these battles evolved into highly structured and chivalrous affairs. Then came the protracted, fierce, freewheeling massacre against the Turks from Turkistan, who occupied India from the 12th to 16th centuries.

Constant duplicity, double-dealing, and complex family infighting finally led to the erosion of Rajput morale and power. The tribal states became mere protectorates and later allies with the British, who began their conquest of India in the mid-18th century. British "residents" were appointed "to ensure the welfare of the Rajput princes and the tranquillity of their country." The Rajputs returned the favor by loyally supporting the British during the great national rebellion of 1857 and World War I, but British power eventually waned. By the time of India's independence in 1947, the Rajasthan royal families agreed to relinquish much of their independence and power in exchange for generous pensions and privileges. Even today, years after Indira Gandhi abolished such perks in 1970, the Rajasthanis still hold the descendants of the ancient Rajputs in high esteem.

Founded in 1156 by Rawal Jaisal, a chief of the Rajput warriors, Jaisalmer rapidly gained prominence as a caravan trading center. Camel trains from Africa, Persia, Arabia, and central Asia mingled and merged here; others continued on the great Silk Road through China. Eventually Bombay's rise as a major trading post led to the economic eclipse of Jaisalmer in the 19th century, but this "jewel of Rajasthan" refused to fade into the desert and today still boasts a population of around 47,000 despite frequent droughts.

Many here still lead a nomadic existence, moving with their cattle from place to place and adhering to tradition. The men wear tall turbans stacked high on their heads. This not only protects them from the searing sun, but also indicates the class that they are from. The women often dance during the many festivals—an enticingly rhythmic, fluid sight to see.

THE FORTRESS city is everything it appears to be from a distance—a magical, golden stone masterpiece of walls-within-walls, with exotic palaces and dark, complex Jain temples filled with white statues of *tirthankaras* (saints), each bearing a jeweled third eye in the center of its forehead. I wandered along narrow, tangled alleys ending in impregnable battlements and sentinel towers, and explored a richly decorated temple to the goddess Bhavani. Fierce Bhatti Rajput warriors—"the wolves of the wastes"—worshiped here before embarking on their innumerable battles with desert tribes.

Everything in this shadowy, mazelike city climaxes in the main square by the Jawahar Mahal (Jeweled Palace), where the regal Rawals gave blessings to their armies and entertained the populace with spectacular

Traditional dances and camel races mark Jaisalmer's desert festival.

Historically, camel caravans have brought wealth to Jaisalmer.

extravaganzas after each successful battle. Below the brooding walls of the fort, built of huge blocks of unmortared golden sandstone, is the Manek Chowk, the city's hectic marketplace.

The place teems with peddlers, fruit-sellers, and goatherds with their flocks. Camel drovers (*raiskas*) offer a multitude of enticing safaris to the Thar Desert; the silky dunes of Sam (October to February is the best time); Desert National Park, 28 miles to the southwest, renowned for its birds of prey and huge Indian bustards; or in late August to the Ramderra Fair, a long journey to see the famous *terra-tali* acrobats and the horse worshipers at the Ramdevra shrine. I'd originally hoped to arrange a trip to the Tilwara cattle fair near the Pakistan border at Barmer, but that event was

in March and I was too early, having arrived here in January.

A few streets in the city are lined with impressive 18th-century *havelis*, or merchants' houses, all honey-colored and dripping with ornately carved stone facades, the work of Jaisalmer's renowned craftspeople. The lace-like details and the exuberance of the carvings reflect the city's love of exotic ornamentation— exquisite stone screens carved in Arabic-flavored geometric patterns, elaborately engraved eaves and colonnades, ornate balcony grilles—all creations dripping with sculpted sumptuousness and bathed in a light so golden it seems to glow from within the stone itself.

Two notable 18th-century masterworks are the grand Patwon-ki-haveli with its exquisitely-carved pillars, and the Salim Singhji-ki-haveli with its beautiful blue cupola roof, but you'll find others scattered around the city, intermingled among the Jain temples whose rococo-like profusion of carved leaves, birds, and animals are even more extravagant. A few havelis are now museums or stores for the city's richly embroidered brocades and silks and carved marble statuary. Their cool interior courtyards are as profusely decorated as the facades—soaring slabs of luminous sandstone chiseled into meticulous tracery by the skilled silavats.

At one point I rested on the rocky cemetery hill of Bada Bagh, about four miles northwest of the city, and watched the sun set. Among the temple-like cenotaphs (chatris) and tombs lay the cremated remains of all the famous Rawals of Jaisalmer. Flute players and tabla drummers strolled among the ancient stones; a herd of black goats wandered home between the smaller shrines at the base of the rock, leaving pink-gold streamers of dust in their wake that haloed the heads of the young goatherds. I can still hear their bleating echo among the rocks.

DESPITE SOME interesting diversions in the desert outside the city—Gadsisar Lake, gorgeous gardens, 12th-century shrines, folklore museums, the ruins of the old capital of Lodurva and its magnificently restored Jain temples—I spent most of my time within the swirl and jostle of Jaisalmer's tight confines. I wandered at will, pausing to sketch the warren-like streets, the high walls, and the towering bastions of the fort. Jaisalmer is so small and compact that it is impossible to get lost. If you do, impromptu assistance will always appear. In my case, it was a man wheeling his bicycle, who turned out to be an admirable guide. He led me to the Old Palace (Juna Mahal) adjoining the Santiyon ka Pagthiya, where royal wives once performed the ritual of suttee or sati (self-immolation on the funeral pyre of their spouses). Then he brought me to a number of Jain temples containing countless hundreds of carved deities in mythological settings.

Speaking slowly and meticulously, as if he were counting syllables, my bicyclist-guide asked me, "Shall I be telling you all the splendid tales of these deities?"

"Oh, no thank you," I begged, fully aware of the endless nature of Indian "tales."

When we parted, he would not accept the gift of gratitude I offered. Instead, he gave me one of his own, in the form of a notion: "Nothing else in India is like here," he said. "You will leave, but you will never leave. Jaisalmer will be with you forever."

TRAVEL NOTES

CLIMATE: October to February is the best time to visit, particularly if you're planning on a camel safari into the desert. Of course, this is India: It's hot and dusty. **EASE OF ACCESS:** Rajasthan roads are rough and renowned for the reckless antics of truck drivers. Public transport can get you just about anywhere, if you can endure the interminable bureaucratic runaround of ticket buying. **HIGHLIGHTS:** In addition to the charms of this remote desert fortress-city, trips to nearby lakes and gardens or camel safaris into the Thar Desert. In Jaisalmer, vendors sell fabrics, rugs, shawls, and fantastic mirror works in shops and stalls along the alleyways.

Nepal

KATHMANDU

A century ago, the remote Kingdom
of Nepal was firmly closed to outsiders.
Now it nurtures secret-place pilgrims.

ARRIVING IN Nepal's capital after a rock-and-roll flight from New Delhi, impressions and sensations smashed into my consciousness in tidal waves of color, sound, aroma, and vibrant energy. I was suddenly spewed out into the living heart of an amazing place—a great ragged intensity of plazas, shrines, palaces, monasteries, and pagoda-roofed temples bathed in sunlight and ringing with the sounds of bells, gongs, cymbals, and all the wonderful clamorous cacophony of Nepal's throbbing heart. I was in Kathmandu's great Durbar Square, ending place of pilgrimages, center of enlightenment, one of the most awesome places in the world, tucked below the soaring, snow-glistening peaks of the Himalaya.

It's a dream—a kaleidoscopic nexus of spiritual and spirited adventurism. I've never seen anything like it. I leave my cab and wander across the stone-paved plaza like a child, open-mouthed and wide-eyed. Everywhere are the encrustations of excess—expressions of the tangled complexity of Nepal's Buddhist-Hindu heritage. Great sculptures soar around me: carved stone and wood, gold-spired stupas, temples, shrines, and arched doorways buckling with age and the weight of swirling

ornamentation. Everything is splattered with red sindur (red dye mixed with mustard oil) or betel-nut juice stains. There are piles of detritus, rice offerings, ashy incense sticks, and melted candles in tiered buildings; white doves swoop overhead, sparkling against the brilliant sky.

It's all too much. You need days, years, to begin to understand all the rich intricacies and symbolism of this place, where everything has meaning and layers of significance (no empty rococo decoration-for-decoration's sake here).

As I stroll around the square, images pile up in my mind like the elaborately carved layers of a shrine: White, red, gold temples; soaring extravaganzas of the Taleju Mandir; a golden three-tiered pagoda; Degu Taleju temple; the octagonal Krishna Mandir temple (the ferocious black figure of Kal Bhairav, holding a skull as an offering bowl, lurks behind a huge lattice screen); the Shiva-Parvati temple; and the gorgeous 14th-century Kasthamanap pavilion, thought to be the city's oldest building. Beyond all this, in the maze of souk-like alleys leading to Durbar Square, are hundreds more temples and shrines.

Everything is crammed into these alleys of hobbit houses, leaning and cracked, beehived

Nagarkot looms over the Kathmandu Valley.

with tiny rooms and ladder staircases, encrusted with carved-wood images of tiny gods and peacocks with decorative Byzantine tracery. Surely it can't get any more claustrophobic than this—a sweaty tangle of bodies, trishaws, street markets, hooting cabs, howling peddlers, wanderers clothed in dhotis carrying only wooden poles and mud-stained cotton bags, and grimacing gods everywhere.

In the misty distance (actually it's not mist; it's pollution, an increasingly irritating problem in the Kathmandu Valley and distinctly detrimental to views of the Himalaya range to the north), on a hill at the western edge of the city, I can just make out the great white stupa of Swayambhunath, topped by a golden spire and the all-seeing Buddha. Here, among the incense, gongs, bells, spinning prayer wheels, bowls of burning oil, and pushy peddlers, scores of rhesus monkeys frolic while Buddhists transact precise rituals on this 2,000-year-old sacred site.

Macaques

Back in Durbar Square, wisdom, knowledge, and enlightenment hang like thick incense. It's a spiritual nexus attracting crowds of fluttery devotees, swarming like moths around the stupas and temples lit by myriad flickering oil lamps. Most are gentle people, floating somewhere slightly above the dusty plaza and murmuring to one another in free-flowing, stream-of-consciousness sentences—always half-finished, left dangling in the air like wisps of hashish smoke.

And there's even more. Kathmandu has two sister cities close by—Lalitpur and Bhaktapur—each with its own myriad mysteries and medieval charm.

FINALLY, I leave. I need to escape all the intensity for a few days. I'm out and into the foothills in a rented car. I suppose I should have gone on one of the many trekking options offered here. These include a wide array of foothill ramblings toward Everest, or beyond Lamosangu to the Tamang village of Thulo Pakha and the Newa village of Serabensi, the Helmu region around Taramarang 50 miles northwest of the city, or 40 miles north to the idyllic mountain-bound valley of Langtang. Or then again I could have driven west to Pokhara and used that city as a base for a trek into the 25,000-foot-high, snow-covered summits of the Annapurna Himal region, or followed the footsteps of writer and mountain master Peter Matthiessen into the land of Dolpo on the Tibetan plateau. Or maybe—had I been truly ambitious—into remote Mustang, one of a number of mountain regions along the Tibetan border still restricted by the government "to protect indigenous communities."

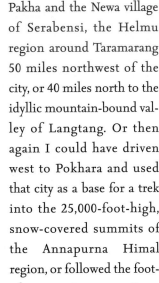

But I didn't. I drove instead for an hour or so to Dhulikhel, an ancient Newari hill town 20 miles east of Kathmandu. Once a center on the trade route to Tibet, Dhulikhel's narrow streets are still richly adorned with ancient traditional buildings and temples ornamented with intricate wood carvings. At around 5,500 feet, the setting was all I could wish for—deep forests, a lush patchwork of verdant rice fields, and vistas of the northeastern Himalaya with a dozen or more 20,000-foot-high peaks rising in icy majesty above the tight valleys. October through March are the best times here in terms of views, but anytime is fine to appreciate the serene beauty of this region well away from the tourist trimmings of the capital. Some travelers come here to get in shape for longer treks; others to recapture some of the aura of the hippie days when Dhulikhel had spiritual appeal.

I came, as usual, to wander at will, to let things happen. I explored the old Newari section of town and admired the temples, most notably the three-tiered roof of the Harisiddi and the exotic Garuda sculptures at the Vishnu temple. My favorite was the Shiva temple snuggled at the base of a gorge off the road to Namobuddha, teeming with images of nagas (snake gods), Nandi, Ganesh, Shiva, Parvati, and prominent linghams (huge erect penises usually wrapped in red cloth).

I sat and sketched and, as I often do, made a friend. Well, actually I made four friends—all big, strapping New Zealand backpackers who tried to tempt me to join them in a ten-day trek through the Himalayan foothills. "Plenty of interesting 'diversions' when you travel with us, mate," said one of them with a ribald chuckle.

Intrigued as I was to discover precisely what "diversions" he had in mind, I explained I had a sketchbook to fill but would appreciate any suggestions for shorter hikes in the Dhulikhel area. So over a feast of wheat porridge (tastes better than it sounds), Tibetan mommos (gooey wontons), and some Newari concoctions that could only be described as mystery-meat stews, they helped me formulate itineraries for walks to such nearby delights as Panauti, an ancient Newari town with some of Nepal's oldest temples, and the charming hill town of Nagarkot.

Their best suggestion of all was the town of Namobuddha, a delightful day trek. I stretched it into two days, starting and finishing in Dhulikhel (a round-trip of around 15 miles). Here I found one of Nepal's holiest Buddhist sites commemorating the Buddha's legendary self-sacrifice, in a previous incarnation, to a starving tiger. The huge stupa, decked with prayer flags, banners, bells, and prayer wheels, is the focal point of major pilgrimages, particularly in March. But I enjoyed mostly the tranquillity of the adjoining monastery, which contains some outstanding Buddha images and a meditation center, where I ate quietly and alone with the exception of fleeting appearances of a young Newari girl. She had the most remarkable huge, blue-purple eyes and a face full of light and hints of gentle laughter. I expected all the Buddhas in the room to join her in one all-encompassing grin at the wonder and freshness of life as seen through the eyes and heart of this young person. On her second or third butterfly flutter through the room, we exchanged glances. Her smile was so radiant it remained with me for the rest of my time in Nepal—a time that ended woozily in a quiet courtyard on the edge of Kathmandu, eating more mommos and drinking communal bowls of chhang (home-brewed millet beer) with a couple of newfound trekker friends.

They had recently returned from a long exploration of the Dhaulagiri Himal region and the Kali Gandaki, claimed to be the world's deepest gorge, below the Annapurna massif.

In Kathmandu Valley a youngster pauses in a moment of reverence.

"I'd like you to meet an artist," the girl said, filling my glass with chhang for the umpteenth time.

"Lovely," I said. I had no special plans. Kathmandu does that to you. Time becomes seductively elastic and nothing seems particularly urgent in this lovely rice-paddied valley under the mountains.

Eventually we finished the bowl, and she led the way past the temple and into a monastery at the end of a muddy track. We were greeted by monks in orange robes and led to a small cell at the rear of the compound. And there he was, a tiny elfin creature sitting on a stool in a bare room furnished only with a bed and an old wood chest. A single bulb hung down on a frayed wire from the ceiling.

He turned and smiled, and the room seemed immediately brighter. It was a smile I shall always remember. His face shone, his eyes sparkled and seemed translucent; I felt as if I'd been immersed in silky warm water. We were all smiling. I looked at my friends and their faces shone. The whole room was one big grin.

The girl introduced him to me. His aura was almost tangible, evoking stillness and joy and something much deeper.

"He was invited to paint a series of *tankas* for the temple here," the girl told me.

Now tankas (or *thangkas*) are one of the major art forms of Nepal's strange blending of Buddhist and Hindu faiths. They are a written record, usually composed in circular mandala form, depicting the lives, deeds, and incarnations of the various deities and the supreme power of Brahman, the metaphysical absolute, the beginning and the end. They are works of the most exquisite detail painted with tiny brushes and using natural dyes made from cinnabar, lapis-colored flower petals, and gold dust. While the broad themes are constant, artists are given unlimited freedom to interpret all the various facets of Buddhism's four truths—pain, suffering, desire, and nirvana—and all the entangled attributes and activities of the deities—erotic, comic, cruel, demonic, loving, and lethargic (the gods are often appealingly human in their foibles).

Slowly, almost shyly, he turned the canvas toward us.

It exploded with color—bright emerald green mountains, golden-edged clouds, pink and sapphire-blue lotus blossoms, curling traceries of leaves, haloed gods, some black and fierce, some with elephant's faces, others with huge mouths and horns with long-fingered upraised palms and gentle almond-shaped eyes, and all clad in meticulously detailed robes. There were scores of separate images, each one tingling with symbolic gestures that I couldn't begin to comprehend. And yet the painting could be enjoyed separately for the sheer joy and energy it exuded.

We thanked the artist, his smile felt to be warming my shoulders as we left the cell.

MY LAST day passed in a seductively elastic way and nothing seemed particularly urgent in that lovely valley beneath those towering white peaks.

At dusk the razored Himalayan ridges sliced the clouds into tattered strips like Buddhist prayer flags, then grew flushed in a peach glow. The lower foothills began to disappear in purpling shadows; a delicate hush seemed to slip slowly down from the high places and ease into the valleys. I could hear the prayer wheels eternally turning in nearby temple compounds, spun by worshipers as they walked clockwise round and round the huge white stupas, topped by the ever-watchful eyes of Buddha. Endless circling. The great mandala of creation, slowly turning through all the centuries, ever-changing, always the same.

I dimly remembered a line I'd once read in Sir Thomas Browne's *Religio Medici*: "We carry with us the wonders we seek without us." I sensed a kind of universal centering here in this strange mountain kingdom, a well-grounded feeling. This was a place where all the secret places, and there are so many in Nepal, lead you ultimately back to the most secret place of all—yourself. Or more accurately, a panoply of selves we misleadingly call the self.

TRAVEL NOTES

CLIMATE: Summers are a mix of scorch and soak; monsoon season lasts from late June to September. **EASE OF ACCESS:** If at all possible, fly; it's one hour by air from Delhi, or a 40-plus-hour bus ride. Local bus services in Nepal are reliable, but often uncomfortable—tourist buses are better. In Kathmandu the rickshaws, cycles, autos, and tempos are fun, fast, and cheap. **HIGHLIGHTS:** Everest and the Himalayan chain. Explorations of hill resorts and quieter areas within easy reach of Kathmandu. Dhulikhel, one of many such places, is a lovely old Newari town and hill resort.

Pastoral Enclaves

Fog relinquishes its hold of Saint-Cirq Lapopie, France.

United States

SEELEY-SWAN VALLEY

Bounded by soaring peaks,
the Seeley-Swan Valley emits tranquility
and the occasional cry of a loon.

I KNOW this place. A sense of déjà vu tells me I've been here before, and yet this is my first venture into Montana. So, what's going on? A resurrected dreamscape in this place of small, sun-dappled lakes set among rolling hills of larch, fir, aspen, and birch against a backdrop of 10,000-foot-high peaks? There is a silence here so intense you can almost hear the lake reeds growing. Then—a cry.

It's one of nature's most evocative wailing cries. You can hear it echo throughout the forest and along the lake edges, over the little rock coves—the cry of the loon. Some say its more like a wolf howl—eerie, haunting, full of ghostly wildness, full of warning. The reclusive loon resents intruders even to the point of abandoning its nest and eggs. It seeks peace and tranquility, and values these qualities above all else, which is also why I'm here. It's why I've sought out this quiet part of Montana along the Seeley-Swan Valley, away from the clamor and chic of Flathead Lake and Bigfork.

Got it! Now I remember. It's On Golden Pond—of course—the Fonda/Hepburn master-work of family disharmony on a loon lake, with the characters seeking, just like the loon, mutual harmony and peace.

Actually it's hard not to find peace here. A few miles west of the Continental Divide, bound by two magnificent ranges of snow-capped (glacier-laced in some instances) peaks in the Mission Range to the west and the Bob Marshall Wilderness Area to the east, a necklace of quiet, forested lakes lies waiting for seekers of solitude and solace. This 4,000-foot-high valley is regarded by many as the Montanan's Montana—a wild wonder-world of boating, fishing, hiking, hunting, and Nordic skiing.

The mountains and wildlife reserves around the lakes and along the Swan, Clearwater, and Blackfoot Rivers are havens for moose, bighorn sheep, wolverines, coyotes, lynx, mountain lions, grizzly and black bears. Naturalists come to celebrate the abundance of coots, grebes, hawks, teals, bald eagles, partridges, even sandhill cranes during their September migration. And, of course, the most elusive species of all—the loon. Experts in loon lore agree this is the most populated loon location in the Western lower 48 states—which of course doesn't mean too much in the way of actual loons when you consider that each pair requires at least three square miles of unmolested territory during their May-through-June nesting season.

Old-man's beard invades a Douglas fir forest.

The Mission Range, at 9,000 feet, dwarfs St. Ignatius.

The visitors book in my Tamaracks Resort lakeside cabin on Seeley Lake suggests others have also found seclusion here:

"I've been dreaming and fantasizing about a place like this all my life."

"It's a slice of heaven right here on Earth."

"When you can see fish 30 feet down in clear water, you know you've found nirvana!"

And talking about fish. That's another lure of this remote valley known for the abundance of its trout (cutthroat, bull, brown, and rainbow), salmon, perch, sunfish, and regrettably, pike—that avaricious devourer of its fishy peers.

"This was one of Dad's favorite places," says John Maclean, son of the late writer Norman Maclean. His *A River Runs Through It*, as both novel and film, introduced millions to the art and appeal of fly-fishing with such evocative lines as, "One great thing about fly-fishing is that after a while nothing exists in the world but thoughts about fly-fishing."

I'd met John at his family cabin on Seeley Lake. "For years nobody really paid much attention to his writing. But once *River* became popular...well...."

"How did he deal with all the attention?"

"Reluctantly, most times," said John, who was also having to deal with public attention following the release of his own book, *Fire on the Mountain*, which he describes as "a kind of *Perfect Storm* for firefighters."

"Bit like a loon?"

Shooting stars

John laughed and his tall, lanky frame shook, "He loved the silence here...the grace of this place."

That is a sentiment flowing through Maclean's book—a sense that we humans are hopelessly flawed creatures but redemption may be found through art, grace, hard work—and fly-fishing! "My father was sure about certain matters pertaining to the universe," Norman Maclean wrote, "To him, all good things—trout as well as eternal salvation—come by grace and grace comes by art and art does not come easy."

And in the case of this region, nothing came easy in the Seeley-Swan Valley either—at least, not in terms of conservation. What began as a scattering of homesteading cabins had by the end of the 1800s become a teeming, tumultuous collection of lumber camps. Millions of feet of logs were floated the length of Swan Lake to the mills at Flathead Lake. Evidence of rabid forest annihilation is still readily seen if you venture off Highway 83 and get an eyeful of the mile-square clear-cuts, some as recent as the 1980s.

IT WAS this kind of land rape that drove the avid outdoorsman, Bob Marshall, to issue his oft-quoted warning in 1930 that "there is only one hope of repulsing the tyrannical ambition of civilization to conquer every niche on the whole Earth. That hope is the organization of spirited people who will fight for the freedom of the wilderness." He then went on to write *The Problem of the Wilderness*, often regarded as "the Magna Carta of the wilderness movement."

An avid outdoorsman and hiker, Marshall was also the founder of the Wilderness Society, which ultimately helped pass the National Wilderness Preservation Act in 1964. The Bob Marshall Wilderness Area, known to locals as The Bob, is a vast 1.5-million–acre expanse of mountains, lakes, and forests and was created to honor Marshall's farsightedness and determination. It is regarded by many as the nation's "flagship" wilderness area and is still one of America's most exciting and enthralling regions. Hiking trails abound here, some relatively modest like the climb to the unique 11-mile-long, 1,000-foot-high rock formation known as the Chinese Wall, where elk have met for eons to mate each fall. Others are far more challenging such as the Holland Lake–Benchmark Trail, a 60-mile, 7-day, ultra-lonesome experience—just you and the mountains, with not even a loon or two for company.

At least I got as far as Holland Lake itself, at the end of a dirt trail off 83. Here I discovered my favorite of all the eight valley lakes. It was a no-brainer. Set in a bowl of forested hills below the soaring "Bob" mountains and fed by a high waterfall at the far end, this was one of the most idyllic lakes I've ever seen anywhere. And what's more, there's a charmingly old-fashioned, wood-creaky lodge where you can spend all day—or a week if you wish—gazing at the vistas. "Every day I come out here and my jaw just drops," John Wohlfeil, the owner, told me, "I never take it for granted. And I never really want to go anywhere else...."

Me neither, although I explored the evocative old ghost mining town of Garnet at the southern end of the valley. This lopsided remnant, once a place of "14 saloons, 7 hotels, 7 brothels, and no churches" according to a visitor in 1898, is still said to be "very haunted." I also started collecting "porcupine eggs" from the shallow lakeshores—a naturally occurring oddity of tamarack needles rolled by the waves into spheres, sometimes as big as bowling balls! While drinking my fill of the local Moose Drool ale (far better than it sounds), I sadly found out I'd just missed a local "testicle-festival" of Rocky Mountain oyster-eating. So I spent time out at the bird-blinds on Seeley Lake instead, trying to actually catch a glimpse of those elusive loons (no luck—just more of those haunting cries...).

You can learn a lot about life from loons, the oldest, non-extinct bird in the U.S.A. and capable, some claim, so they say, of diving to water depths of over 200 feet. According to Donna Love, wife of the local forest ranger and known locally as the "Loon Lady," "they teach us the meaning of true loyalty—to each other, and to the lake itself. All they ask is to be left alone, and they'll keep returning until they die. Loons marry the lake. They seek what we all ultimately do...peace and tranquility."

TRAVEL NOTES

CLIMATE: Winter is often snowbound until June; spring can be wet and muddy; and summer can be busier than other seasons. **EASE OF ACCESS:** Rough forestry roads lead into the wilderness. The road to Holland Lake can be rutted. **HIGHLIGHTS:** Hiking, skiing, and wildlife-watching in the Mission Mountains; and the Bob Marshall Wilderness. Boating, fishing, strolls, and loon-spotting around the valley lakes.

United States

SAND HILLS

You can lose yourself for days here
in a rolling green Sahara with hardly
a sign of humans anywhere.

AFTER ENDLESS variations on a monotone plains theme—flat fields, grain elevators, white clapboard farmhouses, and flat fields again—a single band of low hills, sage green and tree-free, eased out of the afternoon heat. Then gradually roll after roll of higher green-fuzz mounds emerged from the shimmering infinities. I smiled with road-weary relief. I had finally reached Nebraska's Sand Hills, the largest area of grass-stabilized dunes in the Western Hemisphere, created more than 5,000 years ago by blowing sand. This is one of America's most unique and unusual landscapes, containing dunes as high as 400 feet and up to 20 miles in length. You can lose yourself for days here in a rolling green Sahara with hardly a sign of human habitation anywhere.

Back in the Lewis and Clark era of the early 1800s, cartographers were bamboozled by this vast, almost 20,000-square-mile region occupying the northwest corner of what was later to become the State of Nebraska. Adopting a dismissive frame of mind, they labeled it "The Great American Desert." But despite the sand, this is no dry desert, thanks in large part to the vast Ogallala Aquifer, which lies at a shallow depth beneath the dunes and surfaces in

scatterings of tiny lakes and ponds. This is a rolling green Sahara and one of the finest cattle-grazing regions in the nation, with ranchers' homes hidden away in folds of sand dunes.

Cattle ranchers, of course, weren't the only ones who came here to make their homes. Settlers poured into Nebraska by the thousands in the 1860s, drawn by the Homestead Act's promise of free 160-acre plots of land. They came by way of the Oregon Trail—along the Platte and North Platte Rivers—and by railroad, stagecoach, and wagon train to file their claims, fence their lands, and build primitive little homes out of the only readily available material—sod (hence the local term "soddies").

Hardy individuals such as Jules Sandoz put the stamp of human tenacity and endurance on early Sand Hills history. Marie Sandoz, known variously as "The Sand Hills Writer" and "Storycatcher of the Plains," captured the essence of this strange region in her books— which include a biography of her father, Old Jules —by describing the bold spirit and ambitious dreams of these early settlers. But she also echoed his warning: "This country will develop. But not until the ground is soaked in misery and in blood."

Sandhill cranes roost at dawn near Nebraska's Platte River.

Jules was right. For most of the early homesteaders, particularly those unable to file claims near the fertile river valleys, their dreams ended in tales of desperation, despair, murder, and death. As I drove north up Route 61 from Route 2, across the wonderful emptiness of the land to Merriman on Route 20, I could see the last few stumpy remnants of old sod houses and broken clapboard shacks beaten into submission by the elements. This was a terrain reluctant to be tamed.

It was the cattle ranchers who finally won out here. They claimed much of this territory for themselves by recognizing the power and indomitability of the Sand Hills and the perfect match of its grasses for cattle raising. With a mix of guile, generosity, and greed, the ranchers slowly accumulated vast landholdings. They evicted the Sioux, who once roamed these hunting grounds with the Pawnee Indians, bought out defeated homesteaders at bankruptcy prices, and banished the sheep farmers, whose flocks jeopardized the stability of the dunes by tearing the grass out by the roots and exposing the sandy slopes to Nebraska's ferocious winds.

Eventually the Sand Hills became what they are today: a vast patchwork of multi-thousand-acre cattle ranches studded with herds of Herefords and Angus, owned in most cases by descendants of late 19th-century settlers whose portraits now grace the walls of comfortable—and occasionally opulent—ranch houses.

These silent hills are bathed in serenity. But if you listen closely as you wander through the dunes, you'll sense the tribulations of those thousands who came, tried, and failed, and left their dreams in the dry dust of this empty world.

"They should never have come here in the first place. Homesteadin' just weren't right for the Sand Hills. Anyone could see that," rancher Leigh Fairhead told me as we drank his strong coffee by a blazing fire in his home outside Merriman. I'd met Leigh by chance at a nearby store and, typical of Sand Hills hospitality, he'd invited me back to see his considerable "spread."

I asked whether the old cowboy ways were still intact, as suggested by the famous Old West Days celebration held on the first week in October in the nearby town of Valentine, heart of cattle country.

"In some ways I guess they are," replied Leigh, "but things are changin' and its hard to get good men. You end up doin' much of the ranchin' work yourself—just me and the kids. But some of the old traditions are still strong. You should get yourself to a branding—you'll see something most people never get a chance to see—most don't even know it's going on. Real

PASTORAL ENCLAVES

A fence in Sand Hills breaks the endless terrain.

cowboy stuff. Spurs, chaps, Stetsons, lassos, branding irons—the lot. Cattlemen and ranch hands gettin' together to help a rancher brand a year's worth of calves."

I was lucky. I met another rancher a few days later who invited me to a branding way out in the Sand Hills west of Valentine. And what a day it was—a roisterous rite acted out in a wild land; a bonding of men in a ritual of whirling dust and rearing horses and screaming livestock and

scorched cow-flesh, all under a searing sun for hour after hour of sweat and muscle-busting work. Everyone turned up—grandfathers (the ranch patriarchs), fathers, sons, and tiny sons of sons—all in Stetsons, jeans, and pointed-toe Western boots, and all with roles to play in the din and fury.

As the last calf was branded and scampered off to join his bellowing mother in the pasture, the dust died down and it was time for the

Native grassland covers wind-deposited sand dunes.

ritual feast back at the ranch house. Trestle tables had been set up in the barn, and a long line of hungry hands lined up for the mountainous buffet: sliced beef, barbecued chicken, sliced ham, beans, slaw, potatoes, creamy beef gravy, salads galore, enormous fruit pies, ice cream, and endless pots of thick black coffee.

The same enthusiasm and single-mindedness of purpose that had characterized the branding was now directed toward the feast. On and on it went into the evening, with the sun slipping down behind the rolling hills and warm dusk breezes wafting through the prairie grasses, gleaming in an amber light.

AS THE days progressed, the Sand Hills opened up to me in other ways to display their rich heritage and history. Down the road from Leigh's spread, I visited the Arthur Bowring Sandhills Ranch, the splendidly preserved 7,202-acre Bar 99 Ranch, established at the turn of the century by Arthur Bowring and his wife, Eve, a U.S. senator and the first woman from Nebraska to enter Congress. The house and its contents reveal the wealthier ranchers' lifestyles. Eve's sophisticated taste in fine crystal, silver, dinnerware, and elegant furnishings created a miniature palace, by Nebraska standards.

However, the new visitors center reminds travelers as they drive the long dusty road over the Sand Hills that life for most cattlemen and cowboys was a series of tough challenges: Disastrous winters that decimated herds; bloody range wars; rowdy rodeos where legs and arms cracked like toothpicks; and days or weeks outside, in every climate extreme, fixing fences, rounding up cattle, and chasing off rustlers before returning to their shelter of sod.

MY BASE for these and other Sand Hill wanderings was the town of Valentine, a semi-sophisticated Wild West place, generously endowed with Western-wear stores and swaggering SUV-driving cowboys. Primed by its three fine museums, the most interesting being Centennial Hall, I began to appreciate even more the wealth of delights here.

One day, I headed a few miles east to roam the peaceful Niobrara Valley, a converging point for prairie and northern boreal, ponderosa pine, and eastern deciduous forests (so odd to see trees again). I photographed the buffalo (so few left compared to the days when they filled the plains) and elk on an auto tour of the 19,131-acre Fort Niobrara National Wildlife Refuge. I even had a good chuckle at the hyperactive bobbing antics of the prairie dogs in their towns and coteries, or neighborhoods. I had read that snakes and burrowing owls make their homes in the deserted prairie dog holes, but I guess they were too shy to make an appearance.

I then took to the back roads, wandering the winding, dusty tracks linking the remote ranches, and found myself at the 71,576-acre Valentine National Wildlife Refuge, deep in the heart of the Sand Hills. I spent hours among the tranquil lakes between the soaring grass-haired hills, watching many of the 260 species of birds that have been recorded in these parts.

"Shame you weren't here last month," said an obviously serious birder laden with two pairs of binoculars, three long-lens cameras, and a bag full of well-worn notebooks. "There was m'be 150,000 ducks here in mid-May. One of the best places to be in the country, 'specially for the courtin' dances of the grouse and prairie chickens. Fantastic!"

And fantastic, I guess, is an appropriate word to describe this region. However, Jules Sandoz was also right. Much "misery and blood" permeates the history of Native Americans and early settlers alike, and today's cattle-ranchers still face many hardships.

Jean Curry may have said it best. She is the woman in charge of the Old Jules Trail tours and the delightful, memorabilia-filled Marie Sandoz Room, located in her Ad-Pad store in Gordon (childhood home of the writer). "You get the sand in your blood," Curry explains. "I was brought up on a ranch here and then I left. But I had to come back. Sometimes I guess you have to go away to find out what you've already got."

And in Nebraska's strange and silent Sand Hills, each day you've got a heck of a lot.

TRAVEL NOTES

CLIMATE: Late spring and early fall are best; avoid the searing heat of August.

EASE OF ACCESS: You'll usually have most of the north-south main roads through the Sand Hills to yourself—specifically Routes 27, 61, 97, and 83. Adventurers can try their luck on the back roads and sand tracks, where you're truly on your own.

HIGHLIGHTS: The vast "Green Sahara" landscape of the Sand Hills, its nature reserves, and its Old West spirit. In October, the Old West Days celebrations throughout the region.

Venezuela

LOS LLANOS

I was lured here by a famous novelist who couldn't make up his mind what to write...until he met a llanero cowboy.

The Llanos is at once lovely and fearful. It holds, side by side, beautiful life and hideous death. The plain frightens, but the fear, which the plain inspires, is not the terror which chills the heart; it is hot, like the wind sweeping over the immeasurable solitude, like the fever lying in the marshes.

AFTER READING these words from that splendidly exotic book, Doña Bárbara, I knew I needed to visit Los Llanos. The book was written in the late twenties by the famous Venezuelan novelist Romulo Gallegos who later became the first democratically elected president in Venezuela's history. He wrote of true-grit Llanero cowboys; of their midnight roundups (the cattle are too clever to be caught during the day), their legends of the "black gods," brujos (sorcerers), and family blood-feuds among regal ranch owners. Murder, mayhem, magic, mystery, misery, and a woman—a woman landowner in a time of total patriarchal domination. Doña Bárbara.

I packed my bags for Los Llanos. Roaring southward out of San Fernando de Apure for over 50 miles, the truck pitched and bucked. I was in the back with my bags, smothered in dust and screening my eyes from a blazing, still hot, sunset. It was February, the heart of the dry season. We left a trail of spuming dust for a mile back down the track. There were birds everywhere. Thousands of them. Five-foot-tall jabiru storks, a rival to the condor as the largest flying bird in South America, flamingos, spoonbills, white and scarlet ibises, egrets, herons, hawks, and vultures.

This vast plain in the heart of Venezuela occupies over 220,000 square miles—almost a third of the nation—and stretches, 625 miles long by 200 miles wide, from the northwest mountains along the Caribbean coast to the Orinoco River rain forests and the Andes chain.

The southern part, drained by the Apure and Arauca Rivers that flow eventually into the Orinoco, is the wildest part of the Llanos, and considered by many to be the "cultural heart" of Venezuela and the "Serengeti of South America." The land has many of the features—or rather, non-features—of the sprawling, empty grasslands: horizontal infinities, sparse vegetation, and abundant wildlife. Beyond a few scraggly hummocks of mapora palms and araguanays (Venezuela's national tree), the eye

Llaneros herd cattle in Venezuela.

scours the horizons for any sign of variations in the unremitting savanna-like terrain.

During the rainy season, between May and November, the plain turns into an enormous shallow lake. Birds flock here by the billions. Some leave in the dry season but most remain, making Los Llanos one of the Earth's most important breeding reserves and a hot spot on ornithologists' maps. Well over 300 bird species make their homes here, not to mention the alligators, capybaras (almost hunted to extinction when the Roman Catholic Church announced that, as the creature had webbed feet and could swim, it could be eaten on "fish Fridays"), foxes, peccaries, agoutis, anteaters, tapirs, howler

monkeys, anacondas, ocelots, coatis, wild boars, pumas, and even the elusive jaguar.

Cattle ranches, or *hatos*—some the size of the Florida Everglades—offer the only real source of livelihood for the Llaneros. But the cattle are not docile; they are semi-wild and ferocious, making the life of the Llanero cowboy arduous and adventure-filled.

As I continued to bounce along, I knew that somewhere out there in the burnt-green wilderness was a ranch of almost 100,000 acres. I'd made arrangements to stay there for a while in the recently opened lodge (*campamentos*)—a place of welcome and even air-conditioning for weary explorers. The owners had been Llaneros

Flooded plains reflect the dying light in Los Llanos.

Caimans are nocturnal and prefer to live in the water.

for five generations and were hoping to raise capital to keep their land uncultivated and undeveloped. While many other ranchers are constantly planning elaborate schemes for farming the rich earth, and even exploring for oil, this family believed that the Llanos is far too important as a breeding ground and safe haven for endangered wildlife to be changed.

And then there is the connection to Fransisca Vazquez de Carrillo, the inspiration for the notorious Doña Bárbara. Her ranch, Mata de Totumo, is located nearby, and her reputation as a sorcerer still kept most Llaneros well away from the dark jungle hummocks and deadly quicksands it harbors. They called it El Miedo, "The Place of Fear."

EARLY ON my first morning in a golden pink dawn, I strolled away from the ranch and out across the vast plain. At the edge of the *mata* I disturbed a plethora of parrots. They scattered like litter in a hurricane, a hyped-up half-flight of flailing green wings and frantic screeches. Whatever hope I had of quietly photographing the storks and herons by the watering holes was gone.

After my return to the ranch, I was introduced to José, one of the supervisors of the hato's workers and cowboy-Llaneros.

José was middle-aged, with a sinewy body and a sun-burnished face, wrinkled like worn leather. He spoke English and seemed to enjoy nothing more than sitting in the shade of a palm near the lodge, telling me tales of his heritage and his homeland.

"Llaneros primitovos they used to call us. No one trusted us and we trusted no one. Life was simple but it was fun, too—we had our rodeos, played our joropo music on our quitarrais. We didn't need much: cabins of adobe and thatch; hammocks for sleeping; palisade fences to keep out the wild cattle and the jaguars; storerooms for cassavas, beans, and corn....."

"Didn't you get restless?"

"Restless? Maybe. That was the way it was."

The next day the son of the owner of the hato suggested some red-bellied piranha fishing on the Arauca River, a few miles from the lodge. The river was about a quarter-mile wide where we launched the canoe. Thick and silty, it eddied like melted chocolate ice cream around fallen trees in the shallows.

The snout of a caiman nudged through the water followed by a couple of bulbous eyes. At least I think it was a caiman. Conservationists have released a few orinoco crocodiles raised in captivity into the rivers to save the species from extinction. As these can grow up to 23 feet long and weigh over 2,200 pounds, I had no desire for close contact.

Iguanas sunbathing on the bank scurried for cover as we eased by. Colonies of rare hoatzins (fat, partridge-shaped, and known variously as the "fossil bird" or more crudely, the "stinky one" because of its noxious defensive odor), went into paroxysms of raucous cawing when we came too close to their tree perches; they climbed higher into the branches using tiny claws on their wings. Hawks and falcons skimmed the sky in slow art nouveau curls of flight; tiger herons stood still as sticks on the river's edge, pretending to be invisible.

The river had a timeless feel to it, untouched, unmolested, flowing endlessly eastward to join the Apure and eventually the great Orinoco 200 miles farther downstream, just as it always has.

Our fishing was unsuccessful. The piranhas had obviously dined well elsewhere. So I put my rod away and looked hard and long at the river as it eased on, its smooth surface benignly placid in the hot silence. I remembered that Gallegos line—"the Llanos is at once lovely and fearful," and I looked again at the river. Suddenly there was movement, something strange and large out there in the middle, far beyond the swirls and eddies of the shallows. Something black, cutting the surface and then disappearing. More than one. Things with fins. "Dolphins," said the owner's son. "Freshwater dolphins. And manatees. They play here too. Also manta rays and electric eels."

A strange and wonderful place this Llanos, and, like Gallegos himself, I found adventure and inspiration here...and tantalizing touches of mystery and magic, too.

TRAVEL NOTES

CLIMATE: During the rainy season, May through November, the plains become beautiful lakes. During the dry season, December through April, Los Llanos becomes a tropical colorfest with birds and wildlife. **EASE OF ACCESS:** Difficult roads even for four-wheel-drive vehicles. Public transport is sparse; most journeys are best taken group-style. **HIGHLIGHTS:** Llanero cowboy culture; traditional joropo music and local festivals; homemade cheeses.

England

DORSET

This quiet corner of southern England holds the beguiling character of Thomas Hardy's enduring novels.

HIGH ON a surging swell of treeless chalk hills, a frisky fall breeze moved the shorn grasses in sudden pirouettes. The sheep ambled away, as sheep do when people are around, but not before they turned to stare with big blank eyes at this unexpected intruder gazing intently over the hazy green infinities of Blackmoor Vale, or, as Thomas Hardy so appropriately renamed it in his beloved Wessex novels, "Vale of Little Dairies."

Perhaps more than any other English novelist, this master wordsmith evoked the moods and nuances of the southern English countryside so beautifully that devotees come from around the world to pay homage throughout this little corner of Dorset. One brief passage from *Tess of the D'Urbervilles* captured the mood of my aerie view perfectly:

> *...from the upland, to the fat alluvial soil below, the languid perfume of summer fruits, the mists, the hay, the flowers, formed therein a vast pool of odor which at this hour made the animals, the very bees and butterflies, drowsy.*

I, too, was drowsy—the aftermath of two pints of strong ale, an enormous sausage and cheddar cheese lunch that I had enjoyed at the 15th-century Smith's Arms (one of many claiming to be "England's smallest pub") in Godmanstone. The gentle vista of the wriggling green valley far below these open-domed uplands had left me mellowed and more than content to doze the day away among the waving grasses. The bartender had insisted I try the strongest local brew. "T'll make a real man o' you," he explained.

If the phallic prowess of the 180-foot-high Cerne Abbas giant, whose vast and naked masculinity is carved into the turf of a nearby hillside just north of the beautiful village of Cerne Abbas, is anything to go by, Dorset beer certainly has a lot to recommend it. I could see the giant from my hilltop perch, potent evidence of the Celtic past that manifests itself so abundantly throughout the region and which Hardy weaved, often ominously, through his enduring tales. "Lots of strange stories in these parts," the landlord had told me, "Women round here still believe that if you spend a night sleeping on the giant's 20-foot long...thing, you'll be as fertile as a rabbit."

More than 20 years after first reading Tess of the D'Urbervilles, the story of fate's toll on a

Blossoms brighten the Thomas Hardy family cottage in Dorset.

pretty girl born to a poor family, I finally had made the journey to the Thomas Hardy country of southern Dorset. I came looking for Egdon Heath—"grand in its simplicity...that great inviolate place of ancient permanence," haunt of Tess, Michael Henchard, Gabriel Oak, Sergeant Troy, Bethsheba Everdene, and a score of other immortal Hardy characters. I found a region of open moorlands, narrow, winding lanes, chalk downs, and hamlets of thatch-roofed houses with such names as Child Okeford and Toller Porcorum. Hardy country, although it lies close to the south coast resorts of Weymouth and Bournemouth and is only a three-hour drive southwest from London, remains a true place apart.

Thomas Hardy used sweeping landscapes, changing seasons, and the ever-shifting moods of weather as significant and powerful backgrounds for his dramas. He loved the bold sweeps and vistas of the country, and his eloquent celebration of the confluence of rural beauty and benevolence with baleful undertones gives his Dorset a special spirit and mystery, intriguing to travelers. He populated real towns and places with imaginary people frequently at loggerheads with themselves and the elements. Dorset became his Wessex, Dorchester became Casterbridge, Weymouth became Budmouth, Bere Regis became Kingsbere, and dainty Puddletown, Weatherbury.

Autumn hedgerow paints the Dorset countryside orange.

I BEGAN my explorations early one morning at the cottage in Higher Bockhampton, where Hardy was born on June 2, 1840. A trail from the village car park wound through woodlands to a lane full of the scent of roses. On the right, a path climbed up a shallow valley edged in heather and gorse to the open tops of "Egdon Heath" and the ancient burial mounds of Rainbarrows. On my left was the thatched cottage, which sat quietly against a hill that was brimming with honeysuckle arbors, and a quiet inspiring peace.

The cottage is maintained by the British National Trust and occupied by a tenant who acts as caretaker and guide. I had called in advance to arrange my visit and a charming, middle-aged lady welcomed me by offering a cup of tea. We walked slowly through the cottage. She told me of Hardy's solitary hikes over the moors, his frantic fiddle playing at local dances, his fears of growing up. The men in his family were stonemasons, and they built the house themselves in 1800. The seven rooms were small, low-beamed, and sparsely furnished

with plain period pieces. The study contained a cabinet of Hardy's books translated into 15 languages. It was there he completed perhaps one of his most popular novels, *Far From the Madding Crowd*.

My guide, a devotee of the man whose novels have made this corner of Dorset the epitome of rural England, suggested a circular 30-mile route through the lanes and byways of Hardy country. I started out in Dorchester, a busy market town of towers and spires and old comfortable inns set on a hill above the River Frome. Hardy worked for six years here as a trainee architect. But it was as a novelist that he immortalized Dorchester—as Casterbridge—when his

first successful book, *Under the Greenwood Tree*, was published in 1872. Almost every place of note in the community was featured, and he celebrated its unchanging character:

> Five decades hardly modified the cut of the gaiter, or the embroidery of a smock-frock by the breadth of a hair; ten generations failed to alter the turn of a single phrase in these Wessex nooks.

On a hill at the southern end of town, past the redolent Eldridge and Pope Brewery (producers of some of southern England's finest beers) are the Maumbury Rings, part of Dorset's Neolithic heritage. The broad hollow, a hundred yards across, was originally created as a stone circle or "henge" and later modified by the Romans for use as an amphitheater.

I climbed the steep, grassy sides and looked southward toward Weymouth and the Isle of Portland. The suburbs of Dorchester gave way to farms and long windbreaks of trees and then, rising in tiers about three miles away, I could see the vast earthworks of Maiden Castle. Hardy loved the contrast between the cozy clusterings of the town and the enormous profile of these ancient fortifications, built around 3000 B.C. and almost three miles around. A maze of miniature serpentine ravines with steep grass slopes, some almost a hundred feet high, enclose a flat hilltop that was occupied by the Britons until the Roman invasion in A.D. 43.

Thomas Hardy's gravestone

A misty, moody place, it is one of the largest and most significant hill forts in Europe. Maybe it was the ghostly shards of cloud that skimmed across the windswept ditches and grass ramparts, but I felt distinctly uneasy. Or maybe I'd been rereading too much Hardy. Forces of mystery are always lurking between his lines, and I sensed them here in an all too-tangible form.

I RETREATED back to the cozy comforts of Dorchester and found, at the top end of High Street, a statue of Hardy holding his favorite wide-brimmed hat and looking a little uncomfortable with all the attention. Farther down the hill at the County Museum is the finest Hardy source collection in the world, as well as a reconstruction of his book-lined study at Max Gate, the home he designed for himself on the southern edge of the town and which is now a museum. It was there that he wrote many of his later poems and the tragic novel, The Mayor of Casterbridge, a story of one man's search for atonement.

One of the guides at the museum, an elderly lady who claimed to have known "dear Mr. Hardy" well, whispered to me, "He was never happy there, y'know, specially with his second wife. She was rather bossy."

The next morning I followed the rest of my guide's circular, clockwise route through the Hardy countryside, curling around the heaths above Higher Bockhampton, rolling down into the "Puddles of Piddle Valley"—Puddletown, Tolpuddle, Affpuddle, and Briantspuddle. These hamlets, set in woods and cornfields, all have long histories and retain the rural charm that the novelist so rapturously described.

Puddletown in particular is the most tranquil of villages, and nearby is Athelhampton, the house well known as Hardy's Athelhall. The narrow mullion windows and steeply pitched gables reflect the early Elizabethan origins of the house. Now a museum, it was built between 1470 and 1490 and possesses one of England's greatest gardens—20 acres filled with ornate fountains and pools in a cluster of landscaped settings encircled by the River Piddle.

Bere Regis is the repository of the ancient (and real-life) Turberville family, whose ancestors provided much of the background for Tess of the D'Urbervilles. Inside the village church are the worn Turberville monuments and tombs, and a black flagstone marks the entrance to the family vault.

I turned south toward Wool, traveling across the remnants of Winfrith Heath, where clusters of pine and silver birch alternate with open sandy stretches dotted with gorse. In Hardy's day this was all wild country crossed by a few tenuous tracks. Now fat fingers of reclaimed farmland prod its recesses, and armored vehicles from the army camp at Bovington (with a tank museum) hold regular mock battles across the desertlike landscape immediately south of Clouds Hill, once the home of British soldier and author T. E. Lawrence (Lawrence of Arabia), a close friend of Hardy's. It's now a small museum and has a lonely, almost spooky, quality.

Wool itself has been spoiled by new housing and commercial appendages and is best scampered through on the road across Purbeck Hills, which curves over the higher ground, then drops down to West Lulworth and Lulworth Cove, a secluded summer resort and setting for Troy's "suicide" swim in Far from the Madding Crowd. Here the white chalk cliffs of the south coast end abruptly in two ragged arms of Portland stone encircling a placid oval of ocean. Nearby is Durdle Door, a natural arch of Purbeck limestone through which giant waves crash on gusty days, sending showers of spray half a mile down the beach.

Completing my loop alongside the River Frome through West Stafford, I ended my journey appropriately at the church in Stinsford. The Hardy family worshiped here, sang in the choir, worked at restoring the building's ancient walls, and were buried in its cemetery. While Thomas Hardy's ashes were given a place of honor in Poet's Corner at Westminster Abbey, next to the remains of Charles Dickens, his heart was buried here in the grave of his first wife, Emma, a mere mile or so from his birthplace.

Somehow it all seems fitting. Hardy believed in great circles of fate ringing the actions of his characters, and in the old, slow rhythms of life. He understood deeply the nature of existence in these huddled Dorset villages and the intensity of lives set against the huge sweep of the hills and whin-clad heaths.

"It is better to know a little bit of the world remarkably well," Hardy wrote, "than to know a great part of the world remarkably little."

TRAVEL NOTES

CLIMATE: Late spring to late fall is warmer and brighter than usual—but this is England, renowned for its fickle weather and long periods of cloud cover and mizzle (mist and drizzle). **EASE OF ACCESS:** A number of major highways link Dorset to London, but local roads, while well signed, can be narrow, winding, and bound by high hedges that restrict a driver's views. **HIGHLIGHTS:** If you're not a Thomas Hardy enthusiast when you arrive, you more than likely will be when you leave.

France

LOT AND CELE VALLEYS

Clustered around a rocky promontory,
this fairy-tale fantasy has no equal
anywhere in France.

THERE COMES a time in secret-place explorations when meandering journeys and hovering expectations suddenly coalesce into a wonderful frisson of discovery and fulfillment. That's one of those great Ah! moments, when all the wanderings seem worthwhile, when a place appears—a hidden valley, a magnificent mountain vista, a charming, small secluded village, or an impossibly vast desert—and you give thanks for the endless and invariably unexpected delights of serendipitous travel.

I experienced one of those moments deep in southern France on the edge of the great upland bulk of the Massif Central. I was driving along the valley of the Lot River, which winds its way through spectacular limestone gorges beneath wild, wind-scoured plateaus, known locally as the *causse*. Suddenly, around a slow, meandering bend in the river, I saw the village of Saint-Cirq Lapopie. Proudly proclaimed by many as one of France's most beautiful communities, the place really needs no such accolades; it's obvious from the first moment you see it. Perched on and clustered around a rocky promontory, this fairy-tale fantasy has no equal anywhere in France, perhaps even the world.

On the highest point are the ruins of a castle that has withstood savage sieges since the 8th century. Most notably, in 1198, Richard the Lion-Hearted tried in vain to seize it. Henri de Navarre finally destroyed most of the castle in 1580.

Luckily, the village's 15th-century fortified church fared far better. Its proud double-tower profile perched on the cliff edge is the first thing you notice as the village comes into view. Then the rest appears—a helter-skelter, higgledy-piggledy tumble of steep-roofed, brown-tiled, white limestone houses and artists' studios resembling something straight out of a Brothers Grimm storybook. Everything is bowed, bent, and buckled—the rooflines and corbeled facades, the bays of Gothic and mullion windows, chimneys, walls, alleyways, even the doors and shutters—not to mention gatherings of stooped elderly men that I passed.

The long, winding climb up narrow village streets to the church left me breathless, but it was worth it for the vistas of the valley and the wooded wilderness of the upland causse plateau. I sat on a rock at the edge of the precipice and read some of the writings of

The Cele Valley provides wild geese food and shelter.

André Breton. France's famed surrealist writer spent much of the latter part of his life here, among all the other artists and artisans of Saint-Cirq, until his death in 1966. Breton summarized his love for this little place as follows: "Beyond any other site of Europe or the Americas, Saint Cirq put this one spell on me—the one which binds you forever."

MY JOURNEY had actually begun earlier that morning in Cahors, the compact capital of Quercy province, encrusted with bold and bulky walls, towers, and domes. Set on a sloping cliff-bound peninsula above a great loop in the Lot River, the city was originally founded as the Gallo-Roman town of Divona, and was renowned then for the quality of its linen cloth and "black wine" made from local Malbec grapes. Cahors was an opulent and sophisticated city until the end of the Roman Empire. Then, it was occupied sequentially by the Visigoths, the Moors, and the English, and finally decimated, just like Saint-Cirq, in 1580 by the notoriously destructive Henri de Navarre. The place never fully recovered. Even today, despite its medieval charms in the form of fragments of fortifications and gates, the magnificent seven-arched and three-towered Pont Valentré, and a shadowy, wriggle-alleyed Old Town east of the main street of Boulevard Gambetta, Cahors seems oddly bruised and reclusive. Even though it boasts excellent museums, a lively market, bounteous foods—including the regional staples of foie gras, truffles, confit, and cassoulet—the city rarely exhibits that sense of joie de vivre and flurried activity so characteristic of France's other historic regional capitals. Even the 13th-century cathedral of St.-Étienne, hidden deep in the heart of Old Town, looks more like a craggy, indomitable fortress than a church. It is relieved only by the magnificent 16th-century tympanum and the elegant 16th-century Gothic cloisters.

Directly opposite the cathedral, however, is a place that uplifts the spirit indeed. Valette is a wonder-world of Quercy delicacies: foie gras in a multitude of forms, rillettes, pâtés, *civet de canard*, plus a remarkable range of those local black wines for which Cahors is renowned. I talked to a charming young shop assistant here about possible exploratory routes in the region.

French farmer

"Well," she said as she offered me a generous platter of pâté samples, "the Dordogne Valley and the unusual town of Rocamadour to the north of here are very lovely in the quiet times, but in the summer—*merde!* Terrible! You can hardly move. Also over to the west, closer to the coast between Niort and La Rochelle, is a very interesting, almost surreal place, a strange flat area of marshes and canals and little river villages—the Marais Poitevin. But, a few years ago there was a hurricane, and it destroyed many trees, and I think maybe it's not so pretty now…maybe… ."

I was scribbling notes, stuffing pâté samples into my mouth, nodding and smiling all at the same time. "I'm looking for somewhere special—very beautiful but without too many tourists."

She immediately laughed "Pouf!—well—you are here! Right now! We have a wonderful drive you can take up the Valley of the Lot River to Figeac, then come back through the Valley of the Cele…its about 160 kilometers (100 miles), and you possibly need at least two days to see it slowly, but it's so beautiful and not so many people come around at all…."

So that's how I came to Saint-Cirq on that sunny morning in late spring. I followed the lazy curves of the Lot River eastward on the winding D662, passing through a valley of increasingly dramatic vertical cliffs—gleaming white limestone hundreds of feet high, streaked with striations of black moss. The contrasts among the rich fertility of sheep-dotted water meadows and lush woodlands, the stark, soaring cliffs, and the ominous, seemingly impregnable dwarf-juniper, scrub-oak, and chestnut forests of the high causse plateau above the valley, gave the region an otherworldly feel.

The sensation I had at Saint-Cirq—of entering some kind of mystical fantasyland wrapped in legends and ancient superstitious—grew as I continued east. Cénevières appeared with its 13th-century château and troglodyte village carved in cliffs across the river. Then came the pretty cluster of Cajarc with its Musée

Georges-Pompidou (the late French President once had a house here); the huge ruined fortress of Monbun-les-Bains; and yet another fairy-tale castle at Larroque-Toirac, rebuilt after its destruction by the English in the 14th century.

Sixteen miles farther on, the commercial intensity of Figeac came as something of an unexpected—and undesired—reality check. At first glance the profusion of megastores and light industrial plants made me want to swing round and scoot on back to my fantasyland down the valley.

I'm glad I didn't.

Once through the contemporary clutter of the outskirts, I found myself in the town's delightfully medieval heart—a maze of labyrinthine alleys lined with 14th- and 15th-century buildings of soft beige sandstone. I wandered past the 11th-century church of St. Sauveur, a minor feature on one of the great Pilgrim Roads to Santiago de Compostela in northwestern Spain. Close by I paused to sketch the imposing 13th-century Hôtel de la Monnaie, once a mint, and now the tourist office.

Then I strolled on to the birthplace of Jean-François Champollion (1790-1832), now a museum celebrating his translation of Egyptian hieroglyphics using the inscriptions on the famous Rosetta Stone. Rightfully proud of its famed Egyptologist, the town has paved an adjoining courtyard with a much-enlarged copy of the stone, its trilingual inscriptions meticulously reproduced.

The barman in a nearby café was obviously tired of talking about the stone with curious outsiders; he seemed far more concerned about feeding me. A beguiling list of daily specials was scrawled in white chalk on a blackboard above the bar. "I think I'll have the confit de canard..." I said.

"Cèst fini."

"How about the cassoulet Quercy avec..."

"Fini."

"Poulet a la Figeac avec pommes frites...?"

"Fini."

I gave up and asked him for a suggestion.

"Omelette. Au jambon."

"Avec pommes frites?"

"Non. Pommes fini."

So I waited miserably for his lousy ham omelette. But—surprise! What came out of his cupboard-size kitchen was actually one of the most succulent and satisfying omelettes I've ever tasted. Every mouthful melted into an array of rich, intense flavors.

Out of the corner of my eye, I could see him pretending to wash glasses while watching me out of the corner of his eye. "Trés magnifique!" I proclaimed as I reluctantly downed the last mouthful. He shrugged as if compliments were already assumed. A look of sly complacency on his face said it all. But I still think he was pleased.

FOLLOWING A delightful overnight in Figeac and an evening stroll through its ancient, shadowy alleys, I left the town in the mists of early morning and soon came to the turnoff for the D41, which winds westward along the Cele Valley. Once again, driving along this narrow road, I entered fantasyland.

There were more clusters of troglodyte cave dwellings and, high on the cliffs, simple houses with steep-pitched roofs using the precipice as their rear wall. Small signs suggested enticing diversions to grottoes in this cave-laced limestone region. (One larger sign near

Tranquil days pass in the Lot Valley, France.

Sauliac-sur-Cele promoted an outdoor "living museum" of 19th-century farming techniques and implements.) The village itself clings to enormous overhanging cliffs. Some of the higher cave dwellings were once accessible only by ladders and hauled baskets—invaluable for the local 14th- and 15th-century populace during the seemingly endless skirmishes of the Hundred Years War.

Twelve miles west of Figeac, Espagnac-Ste.-Eulalie contains the imposing ruins of the 17th-century priory of Val-Paradis (an appropriate description of the region). A few miles farther down is the elegant Benedictine abbey of Marcilhac. Here the valley became even more lush and fertile with vineyards and tiny plots of corn, sunflowers, and tobacco.

The most prominent site, as the valley widens in its westward flow to join the Lot at Conduché, are the ruins of Devil's Castle at Cabrerets. It impressively clings to the formidable Rochecourbe cliff, giving a feeling of

tenacity and history. Locally known as the Castle of the English, it served as a perfect aerie for their constant pillage-and-plunder sorties during the Hundred Years War.

"I think the locals like us a little better now," said a plump, red-cheeked Englishman I met by chance on the edge of Cabrerets's enormous natural rockbound amphitheater. "I've been living here in this village for over 20 years. We call this our Lost Valley, and we certainly try to keep it that way...never had a rude word said to me here...at least not one I could understand, despite all the damage we Brits did round these parts 500 years back."

"Oh—I've had plenty of rude words said to me!" chortled Bertrand Chenu—Cabrerets's artist-sculptor and creator-extraordinaire. "Oh, yes. So many times when they stop to see my works. I can hear them—'he's crazy, he's a madman.'" I had paused to explore Bertrand's fascinating Le Petit Musée de l'Insolite located east of the town. It's a bizarre and distinctly idiosyncratic chaos of sculpture from found objects that straggles along the cliffside and through his sprawling studio-exhibition space.

Now the spirit of fairy-tale fantasy flared once again as I looked on, amazed and inspired.

Houses perched on cliffs gain a spectacular view of Cele Valley.

Nothing had been wasted. Old motorbikes and bicycles, springs, helmets, old tools, tin cans, driftwood, shells, bits of cars, old shoes, discarded clothing—all turned into life-size constructions. He'd even created a "Parque Zoologique" full of the most bizarre assembled creature-sculptures.

"So what do you think? Am I mad?" His small blackberry eyes gleaming, gave me no time to answer. "Of course I am. I'm a totally free man which is obviously crazy and I have no limits except my own imagination! I produce the best things I can in one of the best places in the world!"

Something that André Breton wrote on his life in Saint-Cirq came to mind: "Every morning when I get up, I have the impression of contemplating through my window the very best of art, nature, and life!"

Without knowing I would, I gave Bertrand a big bear hug. "Thank God for madmen like you!" I shouted. "The world—particularly this magical, unreal part of France—needs all the madmen it can get!"

Portugal
ALENTEJO

A rolling landscape where forests of cork,
chestnut, and olives stretch endlessly
in all directions.

I WAS deep in a silent, empty land. I could see nothing except more miles of cork trees and hear nothing but the sound of breezes among the topmost leaves. It was a hot day. I sat with my back against the soft bark of a cork tree, dozing after a lunch of fresh-baked bread, thin slices of presunto (smoked ham), and sharp green olives. For dessert, I enjoyed large chunks of ewe's-milk cheese. At my side lay a bottle of red Borba wine, not unlike a light Bordeaux. There wasn't much left. I was thirsty. I was also a little sleepy after strolling for miles through the endless parklike landscape of the forests. There were no walls. The grass and the trees faded away to shimmering horizons, and I walked and walked as if in a dream. I saw no one, not even one of the famous black pigs supposed to graze these pastures. They say there is no shade in the Alentejo, but I found plenty.

I had been warned. "Alentejo's a bit quiet and out of the way, particularly Alto Alentejo," a friend had advised when I was planning my trip to Portugal. "Why not stay in Lisbon for a few days, sample the ports in Porto, then head straight south to the Algarve coast—for fun, sun, and seafood, and a little sin!"

"And crowds," I ventured.

"Well, you can't have everything," he said.

He was wrong. I indeed had everything. I had bica (thick and strong) history here in Alta Alentejo from scattered 5,000-year-old dolmen and cromlechs and Roman ruins to Moorish-occupation architecture, heavily fortified 12th-century castles, and all the rich rococo extravagance of Portuguese Manueline churches, palaces, and manor houses. I also had magnificent white-walled cities.

Compared with other northern regions of Portugal with their writhing mountain ranges, broken valleys, and tiny tight-walled small-holdings, the Alto Alentejo is a mildly rolling landscape, where forests of cork, chestnut, and olives stretch endlessly in all directions. Towns and villages are rare. The "monte" system is still in existence, although recent political changes since the 1974 revolution have brought about considerable alteration in this almost feudal landowner/worker relationship. Large farm-houses complete with heraldic shields and baronial dining halls, however, are still the focus for clusters of whitewashed dwellings housing worker families.

A hundred years ago, this was a scorched, scrub-covered wasteland with patchy

The branches of Alentejo's stripped cork trees bend like wavy hair.

cultivation only along the erratic streams and rivers. Today it is a wealthy region supplying two thirds of the world's cork, thousands of sheep and pigs, abundant rice and wheat in the southern sectors, and the great bulls of the Tejo River plains watched over by cowboy-like *campinos* on their Arabian stallions.

I meandered the back roads into lush forests speckled with country inns serving venison and boar—and bread. Lots and lots of it in this land of bread—aromatic bread-and-herb soups, bread and game stews, bread doused in port for dessert, and, of course, big fat hunks of fresh bread in every meal.

Then I had elegant churches and towns built almost entirely of marble. And best of all,

I had castles—magnificent restorations of medieval fortresses, some now operating as *pousadas* (government-sponsored luxury accommodations) and *solares* (elegant manor houses).

The Alentejo resounds with history. Many of its walled towns and fortress-castles were used originally as defensive bulwarks against Moorish invasions from northern Africa and, following the expulsion of the Moors in the 13th century, against land-hungry Spaniards led by Philip II in the late 16th-century.

MY RANDOM cork-forest wanderings ended abruptly 90 miles or so southeast of Lisbon in the old Roman city of "Liberalitas Julia"— today known as Évora. This is one of the most beautiful and architecturally significant cities in Portugal, now undergoing a long-term restoration program under UNESCO World Heritage site protection. Its pousada was not a castle but a 15th-century convent. However, it certainly looked like a castle, and although the rooms (the original convent cells) were a little on the small side, they were crammed with enough regal furnishings to delight any traveler.

Évora is a miniature melting pot of architectural influences, from Gothic, Manueline, and Moorish to classic Renaissance and baroque. Tightly packed within its high walls, the center is a maze of narrow, sinuous streets curling downhill from the remnants of the Roman temple of Diana, adjoining the pousada, to Giraldo Square and the 12th-century cathedral with its famed Museum of Sacred Art.

I spent most of the day exploring the cloisters of the 16th-century university and the Cadaval Palace, visiting the regional museum in the old bishop's palace, admiring the extravagant baroque bas-relief sculptures at the Misericórdia Church to the south of the cathedral, and gazing at the blue-tile interior of the Chapel of São Loios. Then, in the early evening, I discovered the most unusual place of all. I'd paused to watch a wedding in the Church of St. Francis and noticed a few guests creeping off into a side chapel. I followed them. The walls inside were covered in carefully plaited pigtails of hair adorned with ribbons.

"These are kept promises," the curator told me. "A girl prays for something good to happen and promises to cut off her hair if it happens." He gestured at the strings of dusty pigtails. "As you can see, our saints answer many prayers.

"By the way, have you seen our Capela dos Ossos—our Chapel of Bones?" he asked, and

Houses nestle within the hills along a road to Estremoz, Portugal.

without waiting for an answer, led me into a dark crypt lit by candles. A golden baroque altar faced me under an ornately painted ceiling; the walls looked most peculiar, as if faced with cobblestones. I peered closer. They were not stones; they were actually thousands upon thousands of skulls and bones, covering every inch of the walls, decorating the pillars, filling the niches.

"Over 50,000 people here—all Franciscan friars," the curator boasted with a touch of ghoulish glee.

Just in case I missed the point, a sign over the door rammed the message home: "Nos ossos que aqui estalos pelos vossos esperamos—The bones here are waiting for yours!"

THE NEXT day I headed 30 or so miles northeast from Évora through more rolling cork forests, enjoying occasional views across great empty plains until, suddenly, the castle-topped profile of the city of Estremoz rose from the olive orchards—a gleaming white pyramid of tiny houses topped by a massive gray keep and unbreached city walls.

I wandered along winding white-marble streets into Rossio Plaza and found fountains, vegetable and cheese markets, and pottery stalls selling some of the most banal creations in brown earthenware, along with delightful little figures depicting scenes from everyday life. Across from the markets was the regional museum, and all around, the remains of convents and churches.

Estremoz is a place for leisurely wandering, browsing through the craft shops with their brass and pewter work (the best are near the old gate on the Borba/Elvas Road out of town), and generally enjoying the Portuguese pace of life from a shady seat at an outdoor café, with regular infusions of the local wine.

I awoke the following morning in my gargantuan four-poster bed edged with red velvet brocade, encircled by scalloped curtains tied with silk-tasseled ropes, and walked across

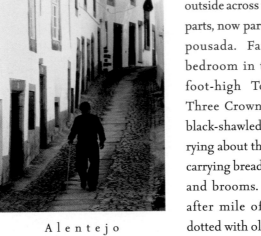

Alentejo

richly embroidered carpets to the high window to peer outside across the castle ramparts, now part of an elegant pousada. Far below my bedroom in the hundred-foot-high Tower of the Three Crowns, I could see black-shawled women scurrying about the small square carrying bread, live chickens, and brooms. Beyond, mile after mile of green fields dotted with olive trees rolled over the low hills and into the misty lowlands around Lisbon.

In the afternoon I drove 10 miles or so to the southeast, alongside the deep marble quarries on the road to Borba. Surrounded by these vast repositories of glorious pink-and-white rock, this is a town of solid marble—marble cobblestones paving the streets, marble steps, marble doorways and windows, marble chimneys, whole marble buildings—all proudly preened and polished by women whose domestic daily work seems endless. The town possesses a remarkable number of antique stores, yet seems to lack that spirit of rampant commercialism that plagues towns farther to the west, closer to Lisbon and the coast. It also produces an excellent red wine that gave me another excuse for a brief pause here before following signs to the adjoining community of Vila Viçosa, with its stately palace and churches nestled amid orange and lemon groves.

Here was the home of the great dukes of Bragança, long the most powerful of Portugal's nobles. On a hill perched above the town are the remains of their 13th-century castle, with walls intact, unusually deep moats, and enormous drawbridges. Small white cottages adorned with potted plants and canary cages clustered near hefty stone bastions. There were little wooded groves and picnic areas with views across the plains and olive groves. White doves skimmed over the rusty cannons. Old men in wide-brimmed black hats sat in the shade of the walls, smoking or snoozing.

The lower town lacked much of the organic informality usually found in Portuguese communities. The streets were wide and straight, and an austere gray marble palace lined the upper side of a formal plaza. This was the great residence of the dukes, famous for its gargantuan feasts, endless festivities, regal marriages, balls, hunts, and notoriously gory bullfights.

The fourth duke of Bragança, finding the hilltop castle irredeemably drafty and damp, ordered the monolith's construction in 1501. It is now a museum—containing ample evidence of the flavor of life during the exotic 17th century, when the Braganças became the monarchs of Portugal and reigned until the assassination of Carlos I and his eldest son in 1908.

After a brief detour at Vila Boim, to sketch the enormous chimneys on scores of houses at the lower edge of town, I continued another ten or so miles northeast onto Elvas.

Now, I've seen my share of aqueducts throughout Spain and Italy, but when I reached the outskirts of Elvas, recollections of the other great constructions seemed to pale beside the towering, four-tiered Amoreira Aqueduct, built in the 16th century and still operating effectively today. Even the town appears diminutive beside its enormous buttressed bulk.

Life here seemed to consist of a continual tumult of swirling crowds along the Rue da Cadeia and across the café-strewn Praça da Republica. The streets were so steep and narrow that pedestrians had to be ready to fling themselves into doorways and side alleys to avoid hurtling cars and trucks.

I climbed erratically up the hillside toward the tenth-century Moorish castle. A little girl asked me if I had seen the Rua das Beatas near the castle. I had to admit I'd never heard of it. "It's the best street in the whole world," she gushed. And she was right—a narrow alley of white-washed cottages smothered in flowers and vines and scores of caged singing canaries.

Shelving my remaining plans for the day—and they were many—I sat down on a doorstep instead, uncorked a bottle of wine, and sketched away until sunset.

Spain
GALICIA

The aroma of eucalyptus from
the forests fills the narrow valleys,
moist and mist-shrouded.

FOR SOME reason the ten majestic *rias*, or estuaries of Galicia have been largely ignored by most foreign tourists to Spain. The British "discovered" them a few decades ago but then moved on, leaving most of the region to the Gallegos themselves. Here are broad empty beaches, golden gorse-covered moors, deep, sweet-smelling eucalyptus forests, and traffic-free islands. There are deep shadowy valleys, mist-shrouded uplands, bands of shaggy wild horses in the wilder places, sea-torn headlands, unspoiled coastal coves, and even a few fully-fledged resorts and busy cities with elegant museums for the more gregarious visitor.

Then, of course, there are the shimmering pinnacles of Santiago de Compostela herself, one of Europe's most beautiful cities. The famous 11th-century pilgrimage center honors St. James and his inspirational role in eventually ridding Spain of its Moorish occupiers. (It took 700 years.) This is the hub of Galicia, a fine base for explorations with a car (Vigo is better for nondrivers), a place to dally in the winding streets around the magnificent cathedral.

I entered pastoral Galicia on a 120-mile drive from Ribadeo to A Coruña along the Cantabrian coast of northwestern Spain. This is dramatically different territory from Spain's high, desert-like interior, the grotesquely overdeveloped "Costaurbanization" of its eastern and southern coasts, and the mysterious shattered peaks of the Picos de Europa, which form part of the great Cordillera Cantábrica uplands south of Santander. The aroma of eucalyptus from the forests here fills the narrow valleys, moist and mist-shrouded. Gray villages perch on the lee of steep slopes. The roofs of the cottages are weighted down with great granite stones as protection from storm-filled Atlantic winds. You sense enduring, barnacled traditions all around.

Everything is granite. Everywhere, in terraces and across the bright green meadows beside the streams, are *minifundios*—ridiculously tiny patches of cultivated land bounded by thick granite walls. The houses are granite, too; even the posts supporting the vines are cut from Galicia's mother rock. *Cruceiros* (huge, carved-granite crucifixes) characterize the region, as do moss-furred *palafritos* or *horreos*—grain sheds shaped like enormous sarcophagi, with white crosses at either end resting on stone-capped, ratproof pillars. The design, almost identical to the type found farther south in Portugal's Minho region, has changed little in 3,000 years.

The music of pastoral pipes will set traditional dancers in motion.

Waves crash against Spain's northwest coast near a lost seaman memorial.

Ingredients for Galicia's empanada Gallegas can be found at market.

And the ocean—there is always the ocean, fingering its way into long ocean inlets (rias) and flopping against strands of near-white sand below bayside towns, where the only disruptions in the cocoonlike silence come from the evening fish market and the booming binges at cafés after a good catch. When the rain is heavy and the ground wet (which it tends to be for much of the year), many Galicians still wear thick wooden clogs raised on peglike stumps an inch or two high, known variously as *zuecas*, *zocas*, or *almadreñas*.

AND DON'T forget the Galician food! I paused at street fairs by the side of the road to eat gargantuan platters of stewed octopus or *pulpada*

(lobster pink and creamy-tender) served *afeira-style*—that is, with a sauce of olive oil, paprika, and vinegar. I was entertained by beggars playing Galician *gaita* bagpipes (not conducive to easy digestion); enjoyed my first *cuncas* (small porcelain cups) of Ribeiro, a young sparkling wine invariably offered with a dozen or so tiny tapas dishes; and sampled soup bowls full of *minchas*—tiny, whelklike creatures extracted from the shell with a pin and a twirl of the wrist (a tedious but tasty undertaking).

As one might expect, the coast abounds in excellent scallops (the shell is the traditional symbol of St. James), mussels, clams, cockles, and even *percebes*, the ugliest barnacles in existence—they resemble gangrenous fingers.

All told, more than 40 varieties of shellfish are found in Galica, along with dozens of varieties of fish.

Farther inland is the home of *caldo gallego*, one of Spain's finest country soups—more like a stew, really—of chorizo sausage, bacon, veal, beans, potatoes, cabbage, turnip tops, grelos (traditional leafy greens), and any other odd leftover bits. And of course there must be lots of fresh bread in the soup, bread accompanying the soup and the entrées, and even, on occasion, bread for dessert: Thick slices marinated in port for a couple of days and served with fresh cream is a rustic culinary delight in these parts.

THE RIAS ALTAS stretch 120 miles or so along N634 on the north coast, between Ribadeo and A Coruña. These inlets are quiet places, less dramatic than the 180-mile-long Rias Bajas to the south, and they are characterized by a pastoral calm. Forest drives suddenly open out into broad vistas across flower-adorned meadows sloping gently toward the ocean.

In the early morning, when mists invariably fill the lower valleys, the landscape takes on an almost Japanese character—an elusive, haiku-like aura. The sharp tops of pines peek out from a shimmering silverness. One can hear waves lapping on the white beaches and gulls crying in the emptiness.

Below Mount Golpillon I passed the tiny fishing village of El Barquero, famous for its shellfish and spiny lobsters. The houses, with their white walls and gray roofs, stretched up the steep hillsides. They resembled the sturdy communities of Brittany's south coast, or perhaps a Norwegian fjord village. St. Marta de Ortigueira, on the other hand, with its secretive beaches, nestled in low green hills

like a Swiss lake resort, while Cedeira, on a long calm inlet, is one of the most refined fishing villages on this stretch of coast. I paused at the waterfront one evening to sketch women on their way to the fish market by the quay. They were conversing rapid-fire in the regional Gallego dialect, a singsong mix of Portuguese and Spanish.

Betanzos is a far more active place, a medieval walled town tumbling like gray lava down a steep hillside above the Mandeo and Mendo Rivers. It was Sunday, and that meant market day. By 8 a.m. trucks, mules, solid-wheeled carts, sleepy oxen, and swaggering women with enormous baskets on their heads and children in tow had converged on the old gateways leading through to the steep, winding streets.

Like octopus tentacles, the market wriggles over the upper town from its center in the main square. Here, in the shadow of 14th-century Romanesque churches and around the bandstand, the stalls jostle together in a chaos of clogs, cheeses, squawking chickens, braying donkeys, black-cloaked lace-making women, and bawling merchants. Hams—hundreds of aged, dark brown hams—hang alongside equally ancient sausages and pepper-covered sides of bacon. One stall sells nothing but cauldrons—great rusty affairs, some big enough to boil a pig.

Nearby, a group of black-shrouded, witch-like women straight out of *Macbeth* were selling soft golden cheeses made in the hills from the milk of their ewes. The smells were glorious—mingling aromas of fresh-baked bread (massive rounds of it), empanada Gallegas, soups with indescribable things bobbing up and down, and endless strings of pungent garlic.

Japan
NIKKŌ

Deep in the misty cypress forests is a small town, home to one of Japan's most extravagant shrines — Toshogu.

SPLISH, SPLASH gurgle. I played footsie with the scalding hot water of the communal *onsen* at my small Japanese inn and floated slowly to and fro as the heat and weightlessness worked its magic on my city-weary body. I had the whole place to myself—cold pool, hot pool, sauna—which was a relief because I had not yet mastered the subtle rituals and intricacies of Japanese bathing. One false move, I'd been warned, such as inadequate pre-pool soaping and washing or allowing the slightest scintilla of lather to enter the pool, could be enough to engender verbose protests from normally undemonstrative bathers and send them scurrying from the onsen in flurries of disgust, demanding it be completely drained and refilled. But this time it was all mine. I luxuriated alone.

Outside the floor-to-ceiling windows, a gentle afternoon shower fell on a perfect miniature garden of dwarf trees, meticulously shaped clusters of bushes, rocks, pools, and elfin-size waterfalls. Beyond the garden wall rose the borrowed view of a real landscape of wild forested hills tangled in cloud tatters and festooned in streams and falls—the stuff of dreamy Japanese watercolor paintings.

I was finally here, in this magic place, intriguing focal point of Japanese culture and history. In Nikkō.

A FEW hours earlier I'd been stuck deep in the steamy, claustrophobic tumult of Tokyo, where the idea of Nikkō sounded almost too good to be true. Somewhere couched in the lushly forested mountains 120 miles or so north of the city, "much less than two hours by train," my little brochure claimed, was a fabled and ancient town that contained one of the most extravagant displays of religious and secular shrine architecture in Japan, now designated by UNESCO as a World Heritage site.

A small settlement emerged here in the mid-8th century around a hermitage founded by the beloved Buddhist priest Shodo Shonin. Many subsequent temples were built in later eras and Nikkō, which means sunshine, became known as a center for religious pilgrimages and Buddhist training. Yet, its significance faded—until it was chosen as the final resting place of Tokugawa Ieyasu, the great warlord who conquered and unified Japan in the early 17th century. Through his highly effective use of power and Machiavellian guile, Ieyasu

Hear no evil, speak no evil, see no evil.

established his powerful Shogunate, which ruled the new nation successfully for 260 years, until the Meiji Restoration brought Japan's feudal era to an end.

His ability to control the fortunes of his ambitious regional feudal lords, or *daimyo*, and ensure the continuation of his reign even after death are the very stuff of Japanese power-play intrigues and legends—which brought contemporary inspiration to James Clavell, who based his popular fiction novel *Shogun* on Ieyasu's remarkable life. It was this vast legacy that his grandson Tokugawa Iemitsu commemorated when he built the nation's most elaborate shrine and mausoleum—the Toshogu Shrine—here in Nikkō.

Utilizing an army of 15,000 craftsmen from 1634-1636, Iemitsu's construction almost exhausted the wealth of the daimyo, who were required to contribute magnanimously to the overabundant magnificence of the architectural monument—ultimately a complex of 55 different structures, including shrines, temples, gates, belfries, great walls, and even Iemitsu's own magnificent shrine.

Set in a verdant valley on the edge of the vast 543-square-mile Nikkō National Park and surrounded by towering cedar- and cypress-clad ranges on three sides, the little town described in my brochure was graced by crystal clear streams tumbling in magnificent waterfalls from high lakes edged by hot-spring spas, bathed in cool, clean air, and redolent with the aromas of bakeries and restaurants offering strange and succulent local delicacies for the delectation of all who venture here. "If you close your eyes you can imagine shoguns and samurai once walking these same streets" the brochure suggested, and promised that I would be "humbled by the beauty of this idyllic area."

I had really come to Nikkō to enjoy the silence and beauty of its national park but, despite the occasional crowds, no one can resist spending some time at the amazing shrines and temples in Nikkō itself. Some critics carp that the endless rococo-like excesses of these myriad handcrafted creations here reject the key underpinnings of Japanese taste and culture, which emphasize simplicity and less-is-more understatement. But the Japanese spirit, nurtured in dual Shinto ("earth soul") and Buddhist ("high soul") beliefs, recognizes and celebrates its own contradictory nature. And certainly, while watching the Japanese who thronged here, I saw these exotic and unique extravagances work magic in their faces and eyes. Something happens here. You are not the same when you leave. In fact, in some rather enticing ways, you never leave.

The whole magnificent complex is essentially composed as a climbing crescendo of experiences delineated by staircases and avenues shaded by towering Cryptomeria (similar to California's great redwood trees) around a sequence of gates, each more elaborate and ornately carved than the one before. Ultimately they all lead to the great *honden*, or main hall, home of Tokugawa Ieyasu's deified spirit, whose shadowy inner sanctuary is usually closed to visitors.

Ryuzu Falls lathers the mountainside white as it plummets.

It was time to explore this unique place, so setting off in the early fall morning to avoid the midday crush, I climbed up a flight of broad stone steps and passed through the front gate, or Omotermon, exotically decorated with lions, elephant heads, and flowers, and guarded by ferocious, evil-spirit-repelling *niosama* statues. Beyond the sacred stables and storehouses, where crowds gather to photograph the beloved carvings of monkeys, including that world-famous hear/speak/see-no-evil trio (another one of Nikkō's enduring emblems), I passed the cistern where Shinto water-purification rites were being performed.

Japanese girl

Increasingly elaborate structures began to close in—the Kyozo, a revolving library containing 7,000 sacred Buddhist scrolls and books; the great Drum Tower and Belfry surrounded by ornate bells and lanterns; the gleaming red and gold intensity of the Yakushido temple, whose ceiling displays a wildly coiling dragon that "cries" with the echoes of hand-claps. Finally I came to the soaring glories of the Yomei-mon (Gate of Sunlight) displaying such a wealth of dragon-, tiger-, and giraffe-carved lintels and eaves that I stood off to the side and gazed at it in awe as the crowds surged past. How long I remained there I can't say. Set against the soaring grandeur of the forest, this unbelievably exuberant experience of fine craftsmanship and artistry held me transfixed. Even the wonderful intricacies of the dragon-laced Kara-mon (Chinese Gate), the meditational silences of the great main hall (climax of this amazing symphony of architectural inspirations), and Iemitsu's own shrine, Taiyu-in, paled against Yomei-mon.

I tried sketching some of the details but gave up and just sat in the courtyard until a kindly Buddhist priest touched my shoulder and offered me a cup of water. I smiled, accepted, and pointed at the gate. He smiled back, nodded in an all-knowing manner, and left me alone with my reveries. Later I was told that another name for this amazing creation is Higurashi-no-mon, "Twilight Gate," suggesting that one is tempted to gaze at its beauty until nightfall. It's an appropriate name.

ISABELLA BIRD, the famously adventurous American explorer, was not known for purple prose, but in her 1880 book, *Unbeaten Tracks in Japan*, the wonders of Nikkō had clearly seduced her critical sensitivities: "Its beauties are celebrated in poetry and art all over Japan…and I contemplated them day after day with increasing astonishment….The shrines are the most wonderful work of their kind in the country."

She's right. But after two days of wandering semi-dazed around all these shrines and temples, the time had come to explore the lakes and mountains beyond Nikkō. I got on a bus that soared up into the magnificent lake and mountain scenery of Nikkō National Park on a switchbacking highway of 28 hairpin loops. For a few glorious hours, I had the spa and hot-spring-laced indigo lakes of Chūzenji and Yunoko virtually to myself.

Nestled in great forested mountain bowls and dominated by the towering sacred crater of Mount Nantai, this region manages to blend hotels, spas, restaurants, ferryboats, and pedallo rides with opportunities for superb mountain hiking and quiet lakeside strolls. I particularly enjoyed the five-mile path around Lake Yunoko, the undeveloped southern shore of the 13-mile circumference of Lake Chūzenji, and the vast marshy wilderness of the Senjogahara plateau, renowned for its unique alpine plants.

Most travelers come here to admire the impressive falls of Yudaki and Ryuzu, wander among the steaming hot springs near Yumoto Spa's Onsenji temple, take the elevator to the base of the 351-foot-high Kegon Falls—a single shaft of tumbling fury and one of Japan's finest—and enjoy vast mountain vistas from cable cars. Others, however, find more beguiling tranquillity in the ornate honden, or main hall, of the Futarasan shrine on the lakeside slopes of Mount Nantai, bathing in the hotel's natural hot-spring pools, or watching artists trying to capture the elusive beauty of Chūzenji from its tree-shaded shoreline.

In hesitant English, one young Japanese painter explained to me that "the light here is always changing, so I must sit and look for a long time before I paint."

At this, he laughed. "Sometimes I just sit and paint in my mind only. Those paintings, I think, are my very best ones."

At one point a vivacious young Australian girl with bouncing dark hair sitting nearby with her boyfriend told me that both of them worked as English teachers in Tokyo and that they too, like me, had been seeking out the quieter places. "Japan is so complex and contradictory—and so crowded!" Anita Blom said. "But in these mountains"—she flung up her arms gleefully—"I feel I could just take off and fly."

Flying would indeed be an ideal way to explore Japan's expansive 543-square-mile national park if you wanted to take in its grandeur all at once. But as a ground-bound adventurer, the key, as in most places in Japan, is to decide on your required solitude quotient and select routes and sites that provide whatever level of peace you feel you need. Select a place where you'll find, as Isabella Bird did during her explorations in this area in the late 1870s, "unbeaten tracks...which conduce so essentially to the enjoyment and restoration of a solitary-seeker."

TRAVEL NOTES

CLIMATE: Fall is the best time to visit to avoid the rain and heat. **EASE OF ACCESS:** Taxis galore. Car rentals are expensive and highway tolls are hefty; rail to Nikkō is convenient, with ten connections every morning on the Tobu Railway from Asakusa Station near the top end of the Ginza, Tokyo's shop-'til-you-drop hub. Reservations are essential. Buses to Lake Chūzenji and Nikkō National Park depart every 30 minutes. **HIGHLIGHTS:** Nikkō is one of Japan's most intense, extensive, and exotic shrine-and-temple experiences.

Epilogue
AT HOME IN YORKSHIRE

This is my territory. I claimed it years ago as a youth when I roamed here with backpack, big boots, and bravado.

HIGH on ancient wind-blasted and weather-worn fells, you touch something deep and enduring here. Guaranteed.

This is the England of the Northern Dales of Yorkshire, where stumpy remnants of the once-towering Pennine mountain chain display surly somnolence, and where storms lash and smash across the vastness with roaring abandon. To the far west I can see down across the velvety farm fields of the Vale of Eden, beyond which soar the purpled peaks of Cumbria's Lake District. To the north, gentler undulations of Bowes Moor, Greta Valley, Teesdale, and Weardale fade into silvery hazes. But to the east and the south it's the sweeping swaths of barren, Brontë-like moorland beauty.

THIS IS my territory. I claimed it years ago as a youth when I roamed here with backpack, big boots, and bravado, battling the elements and relishing its scouring winds. And once again it draws me back—a little older than I'd like, and a little less spritely—as it has for over 30 years. I'm in a coming-home reverie, reaching out for things forgotten, totemic presences, things at the edge of things, feelings, memories—seeking the nuances, once again, of this special place.

This journey back to my wild Yorkshire homeland began in the charming but somewhat secretive town of Richmond—heart of James Herriot territory, home region of the beloved veterinarian who put this part of England well on the map with his book All Creatures Great and Small.

It's good to be back here and I relished the burly flavor and long history of this hilltop market town at the eastern end of glacier-gouged Swaledale. Neolithic man had been here around 3000 B.C., followed by Bronze and Iron Age Brigante settlers. Then the Britons built a couple of crude forts in the dale about two millennia ago, which the Romans spruced up as observation posts around A.D. 50 to keep watch over their scattered lead-mining operations. Waves of subsequent invasions, first by the Anglo-Saxons in the 7th century, then the Vikings in the 9th century, and finally the Normans in the 11th century, drove the Britons out of the valley.

Celebrated by England's famous 19th-century artist J.M.W. Turner as "one of the nation's most dramatic and romantic cities," Richmond is one of Yorkshire's historic and architectural gems. Founded by Alan Rufus,

Bell heather blooms droop heavily in the Yorkshire countryside.

commander of William the Conqueror's rear guard at the notorious Battle of Hastings in 1066, the town of *Richemont* rose around Rufus's prominent stone castle which was completed in 1071 above the Swale River. Despite its broken walls and shattered ramparts today, the castle remains as a powerful reminder of William's vision of a "New England." His plans for this region were reinforced by the determination of his Augustinian, Cistercian, and other monkish coteries who built their abbeys and monasteries around the Dales. They transformed Swaledale with skeins of endlessly dry-walled fields and vast sheep pastures, a pattern later reinforced by the sturdy farms and cattle-and-hay barns of 18th-century Yeoman farmers who brought so

much new wealth to this lovely town. Richmond boomed as a prosperous Georgian-flavored nexus of the wool and lead trade, complete with stone-built mansions and a profusion of stately inns around its market square.

Exploring Richmond's delights is by necessity a leisurely activity. Half the streets and alleys tumble at precipitous angles from the market square to the village-like clusterings of homes and the green by the river. Its primary attraction is the square itself, with its flurry of market stalls on Saturdays and crowds of jostling, tweed-clad shoppers speaking the thick Dales dialect. But the town also boasts the excellent Richmondshire Museum with the complete BBC set for Herriot's TV series

A red postbox is a typical sight in the English countryside.

All Things Bright and Beautiful; a museum of the Green Howard Regiment in the square's 12th-century Trinity Church (described by the architectural historian Nikolaus Pevsner as "the queerest ecclesiastical building one can imagine"); and the odd and intimate restored 237-seat Georgian Theatre. All worth visiting, but for me, the town's charm lies in its winding streets and elusive nooks and crannies.

A lazy ramble leads me along Castle Walk beneath the towering battlements and across the bridge to the river path, which doubles as a section of the 190-mile-long Coast-to-Coast Walk, one of England's most popular and challenging long-distance footpaths, stretching west to east from the Lake District coast to the cliffs of the North Yorkshire Moors at Robin Hood's Bay. Strolling alongside the river and then across open meadows, I paused by the romantic remnants of the 1155 St. Agatha's (Easby) Abbey beside a tiny 13th-century parish church renowned for its medieval frescoes.

An old and bowed man, out walking his dog, paused to chat and pointed back to the town, clustered on its craggy cliffs. "Beautiful i'nt she? Best place to live in Yorkshire, bar none." I nodded in total agreement.

BUT IT WAS time for my drive, the drive I had returned here to make—a loop of only 60 or so miles, but one of the wildest and most scenic in the whole of England.

I traveled west up Swaledale from Richmond along the narrow winding valley road, passing fragments of 12th-century monastic ruins at Ellerton Priory and Marrick and a grandiose Norman church at Grinton, once dubbed the Cathedral of the Dales. The dale sides rose to broad moorland tops, and the meadows were salted with sprinklings of spring lambs bouncing among golden buttercups.

Reeth comes suddenly; across the river, up a little hill with clustered homes, and then a vast village green appears framed by large inns and hotels. This self-proclaimed "capital" of the dale was a thriving lead and sheep center in the late 18th century, and the wealthy farmer-businessmen had no qualms in displaying their affluence with showcase homes. Unfortunately, the lives of their laborers and most other people living in the valley were wretched, as the fascinating exhibits in the Swaledale Folk Museum show. Donald Law, founder of the museum in 1973, has vividly recreated cameos of their scrape-and-struggle existence, rigidly bound by church doctrines. "Looks lovely, now," he told me, "but this was a real tough place back then. When the lead mines closed, people were starving...tough times they were!"

Farther west, the valley began to narrow and the untamed heather-swathed moors seemed to encroached deeper into the downy meadows of the dale. I could sense the wildness coming.

The long-abandoned lead mines of Low Row, Swinner Gill, and Gunnerside have left rubbled traces on the hillsides. A steeply arched packhorse bridge at Ivelet (supposedly haunted by a headless black dog) is an idyllic spot in a part of the valley once notorious as a killing field for miners who died by the dozens from incurable bellon, or lead poisoning, in the dank, claustrophobic, subterranean shafts. The churchyard at Muker, one of Swaledale's most enticing little villages, complete with a charming little Victorian literary institute, contains a sad litany of mineworkers struck down in their thirties and forties.

I paused briefly in Thwaite, described so evocatively in a 19th-century travel book as "a little huddle of stone houses and farms crouching together in mutual protection against the winter storms." Dale and fell hikes from here attract a constant stream of backpackers.

I found even more backpackers at nearby Keld, another hollow of nestled homes at the intersection of the mighty 270-mile Pennine Way (England's longest long-distance footpath) and Coast-to-Coast Walk. Some were here just for the day, taking a short stroll to Swaledale's finest waterfall, Kisdon Force. Others were far more serious bog-trotters, bearing their mud-splattered clothes and rugged hiking poles as endurance trophies.

Swaledale ended now in rugged clefts and ominously bleak fells, and I continued west-ward aiming for Kirkby Stephen and then back on the northern portion of my loop to Tan Hill. I seemed to have the whole vast landscape to myself. The beck far below cascaded over huge outcrops of millstone grit. Curlews whirled like thrown confetti in winds rushing across the bronzed, sheep-studded summits. For a brief while the land appeared almost desert-like, seemingly unmolested by man. I opened the car windows and let the gale stream through, tearing at my hair and bringing tears to my eyes. "All mine"—my inner adventurer sang—"This is my country!"

I paused on the watershed cusp of the fell. Far below the green velvety fields stretched end-lessly, and the ocean, more than 35 miles to the west, was shimmering in the descending sun. I could barely stand upright in the wind; the brit-tle bog grasses bent and thrashed like the coat of some enormous wild beast. Sucking in great gulps of air, my head spinning in its freshness, I knelt and touched the moist aromatic peat—so thick and rich in its chocolaty decay of millennia. For an instant I became the school-boy who had once walked these vastnesses and learned to love them, deep down in the timeless place within, which we all possess.

Charming and quiet, Yorkshire's Dales Country offers solace.

ABOUT THE AUTHOR

BRITISH-BORN David Yeadon's 25-year long (and still going) "sabbatical" from his first career as a city planner turned into a worldwide odyssey of travel and adventure. To date he has produced over 20 travel books and more than 200 feature articles for such notable publications as NATIONAL GEOGRAPHIC, Traveler, The New York Times, The Washington Post, Islands, and many other magazines. Throughout his "Earth gypsy" wanderings, often undertaken with his wife, Anne, he constantly celebrates backroad journeys, secret places, and lost worlds, and suspects that travel in hidden places is one of the most rewarding ways to discover and release our own hidden selves—a concept explained in his latest books The Way of the Wanderer (Travelers Tales) and Seasons in Basilicata (HarperCollins), the first of his Seasons In...series. Yeadon has received numerous awards for his work, most notably from the Society of American Travel Writers. He has also received the Lowell Thomas Gold and Silver awards for Best Travel Book and Best Foreign Travel Feature in 1993, and the Northern Lights Award for a Canadian travel feature in 1998.

ACKNOWLEDGMENTS

The author, David Yeadon, would like to thank Anne, his wife and fellow world wanderer. The editor, Dale-Marie Herring, would like to thank David Rickers and Kayla Weiser for their support.

PHOTO CREDITS

1, Kevin Schafer/kevinschafer.com; 2-3, Geoff Spanner/AUSCAPE; 4, Peter Adams/Getty Images; 8, Bob Thomas/Getty Images; 10-11, Macduff Everton; 13, 14-15, Brock May; 16, Barrett & MacKay Photography; 19, David McLain/AURORA; 20, 22-23, Michael Melford; 25, Sylvain Grandadam/Getty Images; 26-27, National Geographic Photographer Jodi Cobb; 28, Sylvain Grandadam/Robert Harding Picture Library; 31, Dewitt Jones/Robert Holmes Photography; 32-33, Macduff Everton; 34, Jim Brandenburg/Minden Pictures; 37, Bob Krist/Getty Images; 38, O. Louis Mazzatenta/NGS Image Collection; 40-41, François Savigny/naturepl.com; 42, K. Gillham/Robert Harding Picture Library; 45, R. Frerck/Robert Harding Picture Library; 46-47, Robert Harding Picture Library; 48, Nik Wheeler/Danita Delimont, Agent; 51, Chris Simpson/Getty Images; 52-53, Sylvain Grandadam/Getty Images; 54, Robert F. Sisson/NGS Image Collection; 56, Steven L. Raymer; 59, James Strachan/Getty Images; 60-61, 62, Macduff Everton; 65, Jean-Paul Ferrero/AUSCAPE; 66, Sally Mayman/Getty Images; 69, Chris Stock/Travel Ink; 70, Dave Bartruff/Danita Delimont, Agent; 72, Masayuki Yamasaki/Travel Ink; 74-75, William J. Hebert/Getty Images; 77, Ed Cooper; 78, Phil Schofield/Getty Images; 81, Clint Farlinger; 82, Mark Newman/Folio; 85, Markham Johnson/Robert Holmes Photography; 86-87, Michael Melford; 89, 90, Frans Lanting/Minden Pictures; 93, Glen Allison/Getty Images; 94-95, Kevin Schafer/Getty Images; 96, Luis Marden; 99, Pete Oxford/naturepl.com; 100, Chris Anderson/AURORA; 102, Pete Oxford/naturepl.com; 105, Brock May; 106, National Geographic Photographer William Albert Allard; 108, Hubert Camille/Getty Images; 111, Don & Pat Valenti/Getty Images; 112-113, Robert Van Der Hilst/Getty Images; 114, Robert Frerck/Getty Images; 117, Robert Leon/robertleon.com; 118-119, Ben Edwards/Getty Images; 120, Robert Leon/robertleon.com; 123, R. Ian Lloyd; 124, Pete Oxford/naturepl.com; 126, R. Ian Lloyd; 128-129, David Noton/Getty Images; 131, 132-133, 134, Raymond Gehman; 137, Kevin Schafer/kevinschafer.com; 138-139, Macduff Everton; 140, Michael Melford; 143, Kevin Schafer & Martha Hill/kevinschafer.com; 144-145, Kevin Schafer & Martha Hill/Peter Arnold, Inc.; 146, Kevin Schafer/kevinschafer.com; 149, Macduff Everton; 150-151, David Noton/naturepl.com; 152, 155, 156, Macduff Everton; 158-159, David Hughes/Getty Images; 160-161, Macduff Everton; 163, 164-165, Kevin Schafer/kevinschafer.com; 166, Suzanne & Nick Geary/Getty Images; 169, 170-171, Randall Hyman; 172, Max Alexander/Dorling Kindersley; 174, Randall Hyman; 177, Robert Holmes; 178-179, Orion Press/pacificstock.com; 180, Maynard Owen Williams; 183, Bob Gibbons/ARDEA; 184, Robin Weaver/Collections; 186-187, Gary Smith/Collections.

INDEX

Boldface indicates illustrations.

NATIONAL GEOGRAPHIC GUIDE TO
THE WORLD'S SECRET PLACES
by David Yeadon

Published by the National Geographic Society
John M. Fahey, Jr., President and Chief Executive Officer
Gilbert M. Grosvenor, Chairman of the Board
Nina D. Hoffman, Executive Vice President

Prepared by the Book Division
Kevin Mulroy, Vice President and Editor-in-Chief
Charles Kogod, Illustrations Director
Marianne R. Koszorus, Design Director
Barbara Brownell Grogan, Executive Editor

Staff for this Book
Dale-Marie Herring, Project and Text Editor
Marilyn Mofford Gibbons, Illustrations Editor
Cinda Rose, Art Director
Jane Sunderland, Margo Browning, and Allan Fallow, Contributing Editors
Victoria G. Jones and Marianne G. Koszorus, Researchers
Carl Mehler, Director of Maps
Matt Chwastyk, Map Research and Production
Dale-Marie Herring, Picture Legends Writer
R. Gary Colbert, Production Director
Richard S. Wain, Production Project Manager
Meredith Wilcox, Illustrations Assistant
Connie Binder, Indexer

Manufacturing and Quality Control
Christopher A. Liedel, Chief Financial Officer
Phillip L. Schlosser, Managing Director
John T. Dunn, Technical Director
Alan Kerr, Manager

One of the world's largest nonprofit scientific and educational organizations, the National Geographic Society was founded in 1888 "for the increase and diffusion of geographic knowledge." Fulfilling this mission, the Society educates and inspires millions every day through its magazines, books, television programs, videos, maps and atlases, research grants, the National Geographic Bee, teacher workshops, and innovative classroom materials. The Society is supported through membership dues, charitable gifts, and income from the sale of its educational products. This support is vital to National Geographic's mission to increase global understanding and promote conservation of our planet through exploration, research, and education.

For more information, please call 1-800-NGS-LINE (647-5463) or write to the following address:

National Geographic Society
1145 17th Street N.W.
Washington, D.C. 20036-4688 U.S.A.

Visit the Society's Web site at www.nationalgeographic.com.

Library of Congress Cataloging-in-Publication Data
Yeadon, David.
  National Geographic guide to the world's secret places by David Yeadon.
    p. cm.
Includes index.
  ISBN 0-7922-6564-5 (reg.) 0-7922-6565-3 (dlx.)
  1. Travel--Guidebooks. I. Title.
  G153.4 .Y43 2003
  910--dc21
              2001008633